MICROCOMPUTER
SOFTWARE SELECTION GUIDE

QA 76.6 .P467

MICROCOMPUTER
SOFTWARE SELECTION GUIDE

William E. Perry

QED® Information Sciences, Inc.
Wellesley, Massachusetts 02181

MICROCOMPUTER SOFTWARE SELECTION GUIDE

© 1983 by QED Information Sciences, Inc., 170 Linden Street, Wellesley, MA 02181

All rights reserved. No part of this book protected under this copyright notice may be reproduced or utilized in any form or by any means, electrical or mechanical, including photocopying, recording, or transmitting, or by any information storage or retrieval system, without written permission of the publisher.

Printed in the United States of America

Library of Congress Catalog Card Number: 83-60388

International Standard Book Number: 0-89435-067-6

CONTENTS

1. **SOFTWARE – THE NECESSARY EVIL OF COMPUTER SYSTEMS** 1
   - Why is Life So Complex? 3
   - Concept of Fit 4
   - How Much Help Can I Expect in the Computer Store? 7
   - What Makes a Computer Tick? 8

2. **CHARACTERISTICS OF A GOOD SOFTWARE PACKAGE** 15
   - How Do You Evaluate the Quality of Software? 16
   - Software Support 21
   - Operating Characteristics 28
   - Satisfy Requirements 42
   - Software Selection by Embarrassment Checklist 51

3. **THE SOFTWARE SELECTION PROCESS** 61
   - What Do They Know in the Computer Store? 62
   - What Do You Need to Know Before You Select Software? 63
   - The Why, Who, When, Where, What, and How of Software Selection 64

	o	Overview of the Five-Step Selection Process 70
4		STEP 1 - DEFINE REQUIREMENTS 75
	o	The Ease of Misinterpreting Requirements. 75
	o	The Communication Challenge 76
	o	The Total System Concept 78
	o	The Origin of Defining Requirements 79
	o	What Kind of Application Software is Available? 84
	o	Can I Consider any Available Software Package for My Computer? 121
	o	Documenting Application Software Requirements. 123
5		STEP 2 - ESTABLISH SELECTION CRITERIA 135
	o	Selection Criteria Categories 138
	o	Setting Selection Priorities 143
	o	Completing the Software Selection Worksheet 146
6		STEP 3 - IDENTIFY SOFTWARE ALTERNATIVES. 149
	o	Ownership of Software 150
	o	Identifying Software Candidates 154
	o	Task 1 - Keep Abreast of Software Trends and Announcements 155
	o	Task 2 - Identify Sources of Software. 161

		o Task 3 - Categorize Your Requirements	170
		o Task 4 - Identify Software Location	173
7	STEP 4 - COMPARE SOFTWARE PACKAGES		177
		o Methods for Evaluating Software Characteristics	177
		o Method 1 - Inquiry	179
		o Method 2 - Study Manuals/Promotional Material	180
		o Method 3 - Obtain Testimonials/ Evaluations	182
		o Method 4 - Conduct Software Demonstration	184
		o Documenting the Results of the Software Evaluation Process	192
8	STEP 5 - SELECT THE SOFTWARE SOLUTION		199
		o The Decision-Making Process	199
		o Developing A Software Selection Score	203
9	LEARNING AND INSTALLING SOFTWARE		211
		o Loading Your Program onto the System	211
		o Shake Down the New Program	215
		o Use Your Software	220
APPENDIX A SOFTWARE VENDOR DIRECTORY			225

PREFACE

The computer has created the information revolution. It has been cited as the dominant advance of the twentieth century. Unfortunately, in any revolution people get hurt, and the tool of greatest destruction in the information revolution is software.

A computer hardware battle was fought and won in the 1960s. Since the late 1950s, the cost of hardware per unit of processing power has been dropping rapidly. The cost of hardware is no longer a factor in the computer decision.

The battle of computer software continues, with many casualties along the way. About 1970, the cost of computer software exceeded the cost of hardware for computer users. Most installations now spend three to five times the cost of hardware in the development and acquisition of software. Selecting the proper software is not only essential to the effective use of the computer but is the major cost decision in the acquisition and operation of a computer.

The objective of this book is to help computer users survive the software selection process. A few hours invested asking the proper questions and evaluating the important selection criteria will make the difference between success and failure in using a computer. An easy-to-use step-by-step process guides you through the selection process and helps identify the right software to meet your requirements in the manner in which you want to work.

William E. Perry

1
SOFTWARE—THE NECESSARY EVIL OF COMPUTER SYSTEMS

Software isn't one of several selection criteria to be considered, it is "the" basis for selecting a computer.

The purse strings of the excited customer tingle in anticipation of acquiring a stereo music system to satisfy a lifelong dream for soul-satisfying music. The long awaited day of looking, knowing that it can result in a purchase, has arrived. Friends have been queried, catalogs have been perused, articles have been scanned, and the purchasing rites are ready to begin.

The merchant explains the virtues of the woofers and tweeters, the range of sounds that can be successfully reproduced, the grams of pressure applied by the needle, and the other technological wonders available to the customer. You are fortunate in that the vendor has reduced prices for a limited time. Now is the time to buy, and with the technological advances present and the magnificent music machine on display, there is no way you can lose--right? Wrong!

Let's examine just a few of the problems our eager purchaser might encounter:

- o   Desired recordings (i.e., the equivalent of computer software) might be on 45 r.p.m. records and the magnificent music machine doesn't play that speed.

- o   The magnificent music machine may stop without adequate instructions on how to restart it.
- o   The salesperson who sold the machine may not know how to operate or fix it, except for the very basics.
- o   The music that you want may not be available in the local music store.
- o   Etc., etc., etc.

What is the solution to the music dilemma? The answer is simple-- identify your priorities and be sure your top priorities are satisfied. Ask yourself: "Why would I want to acquire a stereo music system?" The answer is to hear the type of music you want to hear without any problems in your own home environment. Obviously, it doesn't make any sense to buy a stereo player if you can't play the music you want on that machine, or to get a system whose instructions are so inadequate that you may not be able to take full advantage of the characteristics of the machine.

"What's all this got to do with selecting software?" you might ask. The answer is that software is the music that you play on the computer. If the software doesn't do what you want, you have purchased a computer with as much value to you as the stereo system that cannot play your record speeds. But records come in standard speeds and formats, so you don't have to be overly concerned about that when you select a stereo system. Isn't the same true for software? The answer is, "No." Software hasn't been standardized like the record industry, meaning that you can easily acquire a computer and while the software exists that you want, it will not perform on your computer.

> **SOFTWARE SELECTION SURVIVAL RULE #1**
> In acquiring a computer, the availability and selection of software is more important than the selection of hardware. For example, you wouldn't buy a video disk player if you could only get one disk.

WHY IS LIFE SO COMPLEX?

When you were a kid and some other kid in your neighborhood knew a secret which you didn't know, he was in and you were out. When you learned the secret, you joined the priesthood and were then able to thumb your nose to those kids outside the circle of knowledge.

Within the mystic of high computer technology are the priests and priestesses who guard the entrance to the cave of computer knowledge. Unfortunately, many of the computer salespeople who masquerade as a member of the priesthood lack the knowledge of a high priest and priestess.

The computer priesthood concept poses the following three challenges to the uninitiated:

- o   Distraction and confusion caused by the use of computer terminology in casual conversation about computers
- o   Lack of knowledge about computer concepts and principles making it difficult to assess the value of computer hardware and software features

o   Lack of input gained when questioning and dealing with inexperienced computer salespeople

Both the computer and the computer selection process are not complex. What makes them complex is the lack of a few basic skills, knowing what questions to ask, and finding someone to deal with who knows what they are talking about.

This book is your survival guide for all three of those areas. It won't teach you how the computer works, but you can successfully buy and operate a car without knowing how the internal combustion engine works. The book will teach you software selection concepts, the skills you need to know, and provide you with the questions you need to ask. Everything you need to know about computer selection, and probably a little more, will be disclosed to you within the next few pages. If you master the concepts, and the final test is acquiring software that meets your requirements, you will be entitled to complete the high priest and priestess software selection diploma contained in the front of this book.

THE CONCEPT OF "FIT"

The key concept of software selection is "fit." Fit means that the software package acquired will achieve your requirements in your environment. In other words, not only does the record provide the music you want, but it can be played by you on your stereo system.

The software selected must fit within the following four characteristics of your computer environment:

- o   Application requirements - What you want the software system selected to accomplish, such as produce a payroll check, format a letter, or create a financial statement.
- o   Operating system - A software package that is resident and in operation any time the computer is turned on which helps you select the application software you want to run and helps that application software move information in and out of computer memory.
- o   Computer hardware - The physical computer equipment that you can see, touch, and feel.
- o   People processing - The processing steps performed by people before data is entered into the computer, and after information is received from the computer.

Unless the software fits properly within these four characteristics, you will end up with a round peg in a square hole (see Figure 1). When this happens, one of the following three results occur:

1) Manual processing must compensate for the inability of the software to satisfy processing requirements
2) A new software package must be acquired
3) New or extended hardware must be acquired

In selecting software, the concept of fit must be foremost in the selection process. Forget the technology, forget the jargon, forget the

Figure 1/Concept of Software "Fit"

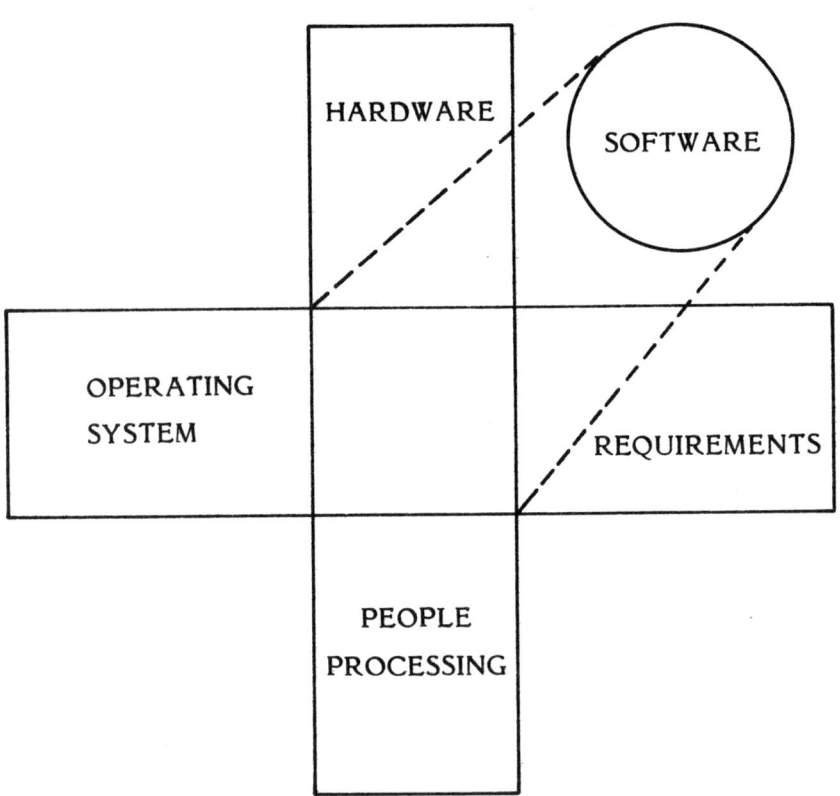

bargains. Just rememeber that good computer software must fit like a good shoe if you are going to continue to use it. Software that doesn't fit your needs will hurt as much as the blisters raised from a shoe that is too tight.

HOW MUCH HELP CAN I EXPECT IN THE COMPUTER STORE?

In the good old days, the computer people used to come to your place to explain and sell you their equipment. If you had problems they would come back and help, but the good old days are gone. You can't expect the same type of service on a $5,000-10,000 computer that was once provided on a $1 million computer.

Today, you go to the computer store rather than the computer people coming to you. You can see the equipment there, observe a demonstration of the operation of software, and ask questions and receive information from the sales personnel.

The novice expects the following when they enter the computer store:

- o Store personnel that understand the product they are selling (ask yourself if the car salesman knows how a car works)
- o Instructions on how to work the hardware and software (when was the last time the car salesman taught you how to operate the car that you purchased?)
- o A product that will operate without problems (how many automobiles or major appliances have you purchased that were problem-free?)

o   Something you can bring home, plug in, and it will work (don't some of your more serious problems with automobiles occur in the first couple of months?)

These comments are not meant to be discouraging, or anticomputer but, rather, facts of life. If you know what to expect you can prepare for it and will not be disappointed. If you expect something that exceeds the ability of the computer people to deliver, not only will you be disappointed but the unanticipated problems may cause more work than worth based upon the benefits.

WHAT MAKES A COMPUTER TICK?

The importance of software can only be understood when it is put into its proper context. The purchaser of software needs to understand a few basics of how a computer works in order to appreciate this thing called software that we have heard so much about, but understand so little about. Let us compare the computer to an automobile to see how that automobile really functions.

Automobiles come in many different sizes and shapes, just as do computers. Some cars cost a lot more than others, some go faster than others, some have more bells and whistles, but they all perform the same basic function--they move people from point A to point B.

The automobile itself is hardware. And like computer hardware, it sits unused until commanded to do something. In the automobile, the commands come from people while in the computer the commands come from the software. This provides both advantages and disadvantages which we will discuss later.

The function of driving an automobile can be divided into categories of tasks. One is operating the automobile, which involves turning the wheel, pressing the accelerator and brakes, and minipulating the buttons and dials on the dashboard. The second function is navigation, which determines where the automobile is to go. The operation of the vehicle is obviously important, but without the direction provided by the navigation program, the car does not provide any useful work.

A computer can be viewed from the same perspective. The hardware are those components that provide the computer with capabilities, just as the automobile provides the driver with certain capabilities. Just as the driver can do no more than the capabilities offered by the automobile, neither can you outperform the capabilities included within the computer hardware. However, like the automobile, the hardware sits there until it is properly instructed.

There are two major tasks involved in operating the hardware. The first is the equivalent of the driver in the automobile, which in a computer system is called the operating system. The operating system job functions are similar to that of the driver of the automobile in that the operating system controls the physical characteristics of the computer. The operating system can make the printer print, the read heads on the disk drive move, and accept data from the computer terminal. It is important to remember that these are just operating-type commands and by themselves do not perform any useful work.

The direction for the meaningful use of the computer comes from the application software. This is the navigator for the computer detailing what the computer is to do and how those tasks should be performed. It is like the navigator providing direction on what routes to take, when to turn, and what landmarks to look for.

The computer without the proper navigator can be destroyed in the unfriendly sea of operations. In computer terms, the inability to continue operations is called a "crash." These crashes occur because the application software provides the wrong directions, for example, instead of telling the computer to turn left following the safe and easy route, the instructions are to turn right over the cliff, resulting in a disastrous crash.

Knowing that you are getting good software is similar to knowing that a friend is giving you good instructions on how to find some location. One would not start out on a complex route without asking a few questions about the directions or clarifications about the meaning of certain instructions. The same attention to detail is needed if the application software purchased is to meet your processing requirements.

Computer System Overview

We can visualize in an automobile the car, the driver, and a navigator. We understand that the wheels turn when you move the steering wheel, and the car accelerates when you push the gas pedal. Let's look at a computer system for a few minutes to put the computer pieces in the same type of perspective.

A schematic overview of a computer is illustrated in Figure 2. Some of the components are very familiar, like the terminal and printer, but other components such as the central processing unit and disk drives may not be as familiar. These are the computer components that need to be understood prior to the software selection process.

A schematic of the computer is divided into two basic parts. One part is data and the other part is processing. This explains why we use the term data processing, and when we consider that it is run by electricity we then extend the concept to electronic data processing or as it is affectionately known in the trade, EDP.

The data part of the computer is comprised of the devices used to enter, store, display, or print data. These include the terminal which is comprised of the screen and keyboard, a disk drive which holds diskettes on which data is stored, and a printer which permits us to make hard-copy documents.

The processing part of the computer is known technically as the central processing unit or CPU, but more frequently referred to as memory or computer storage. In reality, it is the central processing unit that provides the processing capability that will be used by the software contained in the main storage or memory unit of the computer.

Within processing, we see three general categories, which are the

Figure 2/What Makes a Computer Tick?

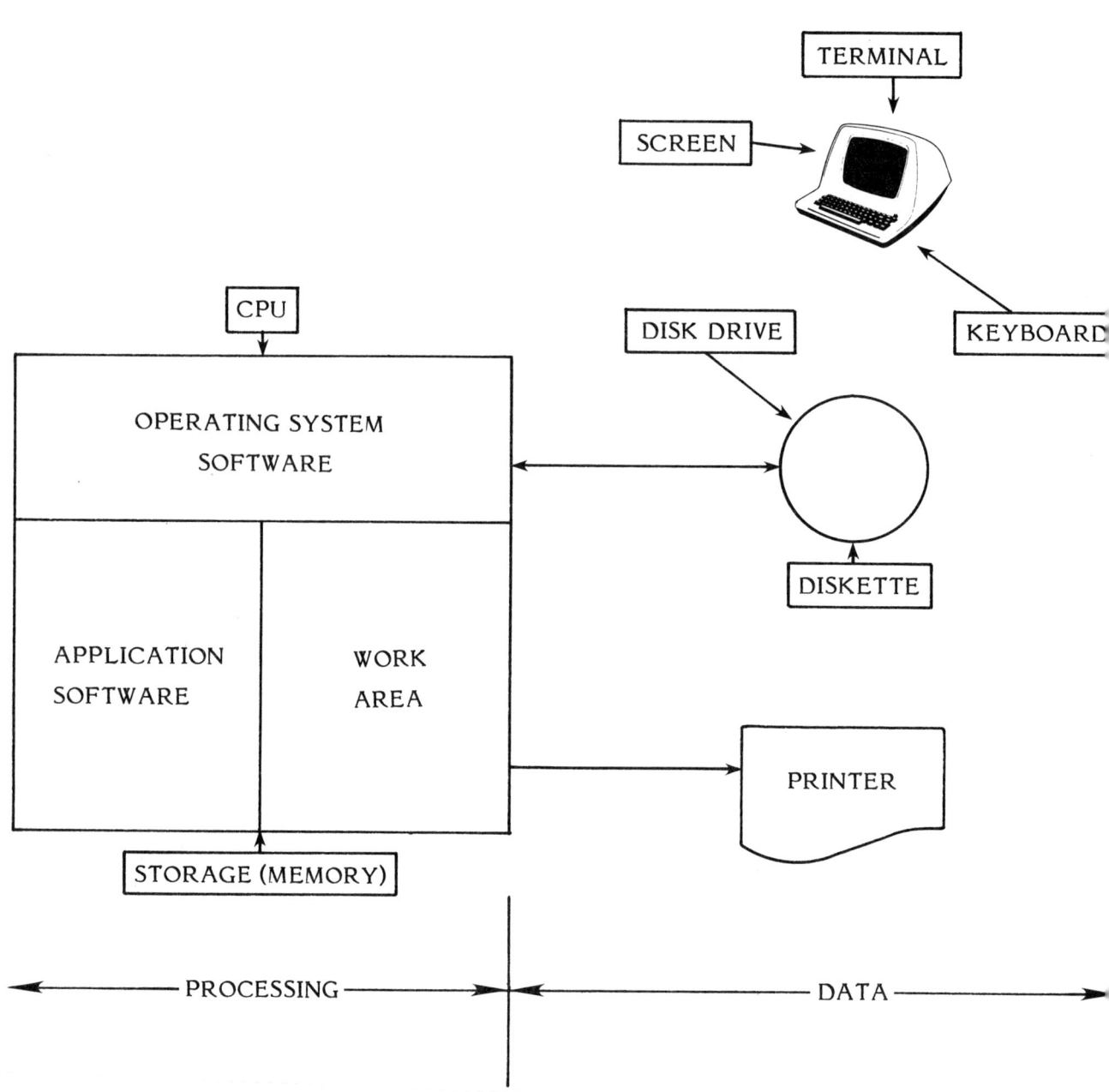

operating system software, the application software, and the work area. The operating system software is normally provided by the vendor that makes the hardware and has general operating responsibilities for the computer.

Having an operating system provided with the computer is the equivalent of purchasing an automobile and having the manufacturer supply you with a chauffeur to drive the automobile. With the automobile and chauffeur all you need to do is provide the directions, explaining how you want the automobile used. The application software are those directions for the computer. For example, if you want the computer to produce a payroll check, the application software would be payroll processing software; and if you wanted the computer to properly structure a letter for you and check the spelling, the application software would be called a word processor.

Computer storage capacity or memory units come in various sizes, usually expressed in terms of 1,000 units of storage, which is referred to as "K" units of storage. For example, 64K of storage is 64,000 units of storage. The operating system software will use an additional segment, and whatever is left can be called a work area or working storage. This work area is the equivalent of a yellow pad of paper we use when we are attempting to solve a problem. The work area can be used to perform calculations, to hold information until we need it at a later time, or if not needed just left blank.

The two most popular types of computer storage are eight-bit and sixteen-bit units of computer storage. In other words, each unit of storage can hold eight or sixteen bits. A bit is a condition which can respond to a yes-no condition and is used to encode data. As the numbers indicate, sixteen-bit storage is twice as big as eight-bit storage, and therefore should impress you, but in actual fact it may be unimportant to you as a user of the computer. I am sure you are just as concerned about the number of cubic inches of piston displacement in your engine, the number of barrels in your carburetor, and the gear ratio of your transmission. Fortunately, most people are able to buy a car to satisfy their needs without understanding piston displacement. What is important is to understand your processing requirements, and then acquire the processing capabilities to satisfy those requirements.

> **SOFTWARE SELECTION SURVIVAL RULE #2**
> **Selecting computers based solely on technical capabilities is like buying a television to watch test patterns.**

2
CHARACTERISTICS OF A GOOD SOFTWARE PACKAGE

A good software package is like a good shoe, if it fits well you'll get years of good use out of it.

Quality, like beauty, is in the eyes of the beholder. If the computer field is looked at as "black art" then the measurement of the quality of software is impossible. To many, it is as unthinkable to quantify the quality of software using a schoolroom scoring system as it would be to quantify a Rembrandt painting.

Many buy and sell software without any basis for measuring the goodness or badness of that piece of software. In this type of evaluation environment, one must rely upon for evaluation:

- o Opinions of friends and acquaintances
- o Claims by the software vendor
- o Recommendations by salespersons

These methods may work but if they do you have either found a good advisor or have been lucky. It is the equivalent to buying stock on the tip of a friend, recommendations by the owners of the company, or tips by your stockbroker. If these methods worked, we would all be rich.

The software selection process commences with an understanding of the characteristics of good software. You can't assume that all payroll application software is alike any more than you would assume that all automobiles are alike. Software varies more in capabilities than automobiles do.

If payroll is a common task for all businesses and much of the payroll processing is specified by law, why are there over 50,000 different payroll systems in the United States? The answer is that 50,000 people found a way to be different.

HOW DO YOU EVALUATE THE QUALITY OF SOFTWARE?

Software is the automation of the thought processes used by people in performing a task. There is nothing magical about software except for the fact that it can break tasks into its component parts so they can be processed repetitively by machines. The magic of software is not that it can do complex tasks but, rather, that it can break what appear to be relatively simple tasks for people into very minute steps that can be performed by a machine.

If you wanted to begin to understand the magnificence required to develop a good piece of software, try and document the task of writing your first name on a piece of paper with a pencil. Begin the instructions with what you must do with each finger in order to pick up the pencil, explain how to hold the pencil and maneuver your fingers in order to form each letter. Don't forget that if the pencil is not on the paper the letters won't be drawn, and if it is pressed too tight you will rip the paper. Attempt this exercise with a friend, in which you give the instructions and your friend follows them explicitly The odds are that the name will never be written on the paper. The development of software to be viable must solve this task flawlessly or the product you buy will be worthless to you.

In the thirty years since the advent of the first commercial computer, we have learned a lot about the traits and characteristics of good software--the absence of which produces poor software. If we find these desirable criteria present in the software, then there is a high probability that the software will do what we want. On the other hand, the absence of those criteria normally spell trouble for the person acquiring that specific software package.

The High Probabability Theory

Most people selecting software have neither the time nor aptitude to perform a detailed analysis on that software prior to acquisition. Therefore, what is needed is a process that will minimize your effort in evaluating software, and yet provide you with a high probability that what you get will perform the job you need performed. The proposed method is known as the high probability theory.

The insurance industry has practiced this theory for hundreds of years. If I were to apply for a life insurance policy on my life the insurance company would ask me a series of questions such as:

- o   What is my age?
- o   What is my occupation?
- o   Do I smoke; if so, how much?

o   What is the condition of my health?
o   What is the health history of my family?
o   What is my weight and height?

Each of these questions is a criterion that correlates to how long I will live, because the insurance company is betting that I will live and when I take out insurance I am betting that I will die. In order to stack the odds in their favor (i.e., the high probability theory), they want to know what the chances are that I will die. In asking the questions, they know, for example, that the older I am the more likely I am to die; the more I smoke the more likely I am to die; the more overweight I am the more likely I am to die; and so on. If the answers to their criteria show a high probability of death, they don't want to insure me; if the questions show a low probability of death, I get the insurance automatically; and if there is some uncertainty, the insurance company asks me to take a physical.

The high probability theory is recommended for use in determining whether a software package overwhelmingly meets your needs, in which case you might want to purchase it without any further investigations; whether there is little chance that the software will satisfy your needs, in which case you must do further investigation. The latter chapters in the book will explain that further investigation and selection process if the high probability theory does not clearly demonstrate a software solution for your needs.

Software Selection Categories

The software selection criteria can be categorized into the following three groups (see Figure 3):

- o Software support - The characteristics of the company that developed the application software.
- o Operating characteristics - The methods and procedures by which people interface with the application software.
- o Satisfy requirements - The ability of the application software to perform the needed processing tasks.

Many people evaluate software on only one or two of these three selection characteristics. Note that these same characteristics apply to the selection of many other acquired items, such as automobiles. If we select our software based on vendor support, then the fact that it was developed by a specific vendor may be enough to make the selection. For example, we may buy an automobile because it was made by Ford and not even consider automobiles manufactured by other vendors. If we select software or an automobile on operating characteristics, we may be overly influenced by the automatic transmission, color of the fabrics, and instrument panel and forget about why we are buying the automobile. On the other hand, if needs requirements become our sole selection criteria we may overlook the fact that the software is so complex and difficult to use that it becomes easier to do the job manually than to do it on the computer.

Let's look at what experience has taught us are important selection

Figure 3/Software Selection Hierarchy

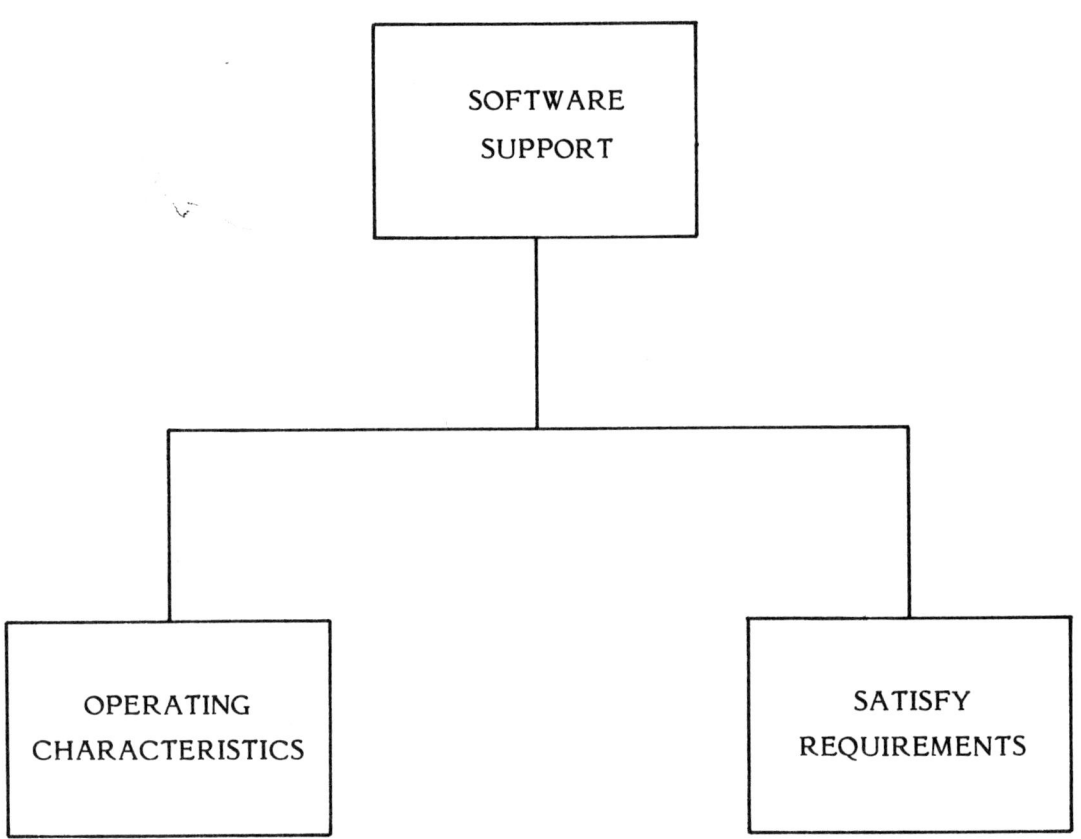

criteria in each of the three selection categories.

SOFTWARE SUPPORT

In understanding the basis for the selection category of software support it is necessary to understand the following software facts of life:

- o   Fact #1 - The vendor developed the software package, not you.
- o   Fact #2 - You must operate the software package, not the vendor.
- o   Fact #3 - The knowledge of how to use it must be transferred from the vendor to you.
- o   Fact #4 - A software package should not be expected to work flawlessly.
- o   Fact #5 - If software flaws or problems occur they are primarily your problems, not the vendor's.

Understanding these software facts of life demonstrates the importance of vendor software support as a quality characteristic of application software. Unless you are a skilled computer programmer with unlimited amounts of time, the knowledge transfer and support are important to you. Would you buy a washing machine if no one could tell you how to operate it or fix it if it broke down?

> **SOFTWARE SELECTION SURVIVAL RULE # 3**
> There is a time to be alone, and a time to be with vendor software support personnel—when you are having a problem with application software is no time to be alone.

The criteria to measure quality software in a vendor software support area are listed in Figure 4 and described below:

Vendor Reputation

There are thousands of vendors that make software for computers. Some are highly skilled professionals who have worked for years to master their trade, and others may be people like yourself with only a few months of computer experience under their belt. You could fill a swimming pool with the tears of computer users who bought software from the wrong group. Many of these software vendors won't be in business three months from today.

A rule of thumb that was taught me about building a swimming pool in Florida is to have the pool constructed by a firm who has been in business more than five years. I followed that rule, paid a few dollars more, and have had years of enjoyment out of my swimming pool while some friends who were hypnotized by a few prize-winning photographs of swimming pools are still waiting for the results of bankruptcy proceedings to determine whether the unfinished pile of concrete in their back yard can be converted into a swimming pool.

Figure 4/Software Support

#	EVALUATION CRITERIA	DESCRIPTION OF CRITERIA
1.	Vendor reputation	The experience and respect for the vendor in the market place.
2.	Software training	The methods, material, and location by which the user can be trained in how to implement and operate the application software package.
3.	Software service	The support provided the user of the application in overcoming detected application software problems.
4.	Software enhancements	The intent and experience of the vendor in improving the performance and capabilities of the software package.

A few well-placed questions about the length of time the vendor has been in business, the number of copies of the software package that you are interested in that have been sold, and the names of a few references may save you some of the grief that is so common in the software field.

Training

Training is an essential ingredient in the success of application software. Unless you are a button pusher who likes to learn through trial and error, the software will be of little value unless you are trained in how to use it. The better the training, the quicker and more effective you will be in the use of the software.

Two types of training are required to use most software packages. First is training in the area covered by the software package; and the second type of training is in the use of the software. For example, to use a payroll application you would first need to understand payroll principles and then second, how to use the application system to apply those principles in the calculation of payroll.

Computer training provided by the vendor covers how to use the software package. Understanding the area, such as payroll principles, is not a responsibility of the user.

Training can normally be acquired in any of the following manners:

- Vendor seminars - Vendor personnel train you in a classroom situation on how to use the software.

- Software store training - The individuals that sell you the software train you on how to use the software. This may be formal or informal training; for example, the training may occur during a demonstration of the package or it may include so many hours of training at your place of business.

- Training manuals/courses - Either written or automated computer courses may be provided by the vendor to teach you how to use the software.

- Third-party training - Professional trainers or other users of the software may provide training to instruct you on how to use the software.

The training method should be suited to your knowledge level. For example, a training manual that assumes a certain level of knowledge may be of little value to you in learning how to use acquired software. Not only do you need the right type of training, but the training aimed at your level of knowledge.

Software Service

Someone must have said, or should have said, "Anything built by a man will periodically fail." Software certainly falls into that broad category of things that periodically fail. The problem is, what do you do when the computer stops? (Kick it is not the correct answer.)

Let's look at the type of things that can cause the computer system to fail:

- Hardware failure
- People failure in not operating the software correctly
- Entry of incorrect data
- Application software bug (a bug is software term meaning an error)

Obviously, the software vendor is only going to help you with software problems. Unfortunately, problems normally occur during the execution of an application software system.

Few of us can repair our own car, so when it stops or malfunctions we require service. Even fewer of us are capable of maintaining software systems. Thus, when the software fails or produces incorrect results we need service.

Who is going to provide that service? If it is not the vendor, it must be you! If you can't provide the service you better find out what will happen when the software system fails, because it will--and according to Murphy it will fail at the worst possible time. Murphy also said that if a peanut-butter covered cracker fell it would hit the floor peanut-butter side down.

Software Enhancements

A frustrated computer user once said, "The only thing that is constant is change." That user must have acquired a software package only to find out that the user's requirements changed. What once worked well no longer works. The house with two bedrooms is fine until the second or third child arrives. At that point, the family faces the option of buying a new house or enlarging or enhancing the first house.

The same options occur with system software. If your requirements change, and they will, and the software requirements don't change, and they won't unless the vendor changes them, then you are sitting somewhere between a hard place and a rock. Sometimes it is as difficult to change from one software package to another, as it is to physically move from one home to another.

It never pays to wait until a better piece of software is developed. There will always be better software packages under development. Some people are still waiting for color television to be perfected before they buy it. You should get the best software package you can buy today, but don't put blinders on about tomorrow's requirements.

Some vendors enhance and improve their software, while others only develop new software packages. You don't know what your requirements will be tomorrow and the vendor would be foolish to promise enhancements unless they are developed and will be delivered on a specific date. What you can look for is the vendor's commitment to continually improve the quality and capability of the software product. If this is the vendor's intention, then as a potential customer you should determine if you are eligible to acquire enhanced versions of the software at nominal prices.

OPERATING CHARACTERISTICS

Operating characteristics are the software capabilities provided by vendors that simplify the use of software and make your life much easier. When color televisions were first introduced there were several dials that had to be turned to acquire a good color picture each time the channel was turned. Today, the desired color level can be set once and the color set will automatically adjust the transmitted picture to the user's desired coloring. That automatic color adjustment is a desirable operating characteristic of a color television set.

There are many ways to accomplish the same task regardless of whether the task is baking a cake or operating computer software. Some of those ways are far superior than others. For example, beating a cake batter with an electric beater is a far superior way to make a cake than beating the batter in a bowl with a spoon.

The desirable software operating characteristics are listed in Figure 5 and described below:

Menu Driven

A menu in data processing terminology means the ability to select among a series of options. It is similar to a menu in a restaurant in which you select among the foods the restaurant has available. A menu in a computer system lists the capabilities or features available for you to select the one you want.

Let's look at a simple example of a menu-driven name and address file. Menus are associated with computer systems that have terminals, and the menus are displayed on the terminal screen as a series of available options. In our name and address file example, the menu may offer the following three options:

1) Add a new name and address to the file
2) Delete a name and address from the file
3) Change a name or address in the file

The menu-driven concept would let you select which of those options you desire, for example, let's assume you want to change a name and address record. In a menu-driven system, you would now be given another menu which might offer these options:

1) Change name
2) Change address
3) Change city
4) Change state
5) Change zip code

Note that the items on the menu need not be mutually exclusive. In our address change example you may want to change the address, city, state, and zip code. On the other hand, if only the zip code is wrong

Figure 5/Operating Characteristics

#	EVALUATION CRITERIA	DESCRIPTION OF CRITERIA
1.	Menu driven	The options available in a software package, together with the processing capabilities, are presented in a menu format as the basis for initiating action.
2.	Usable documentation	The documentation on how to implement and operate the application is sufficiently descriptive to enable the user to effectively utilize the software package features.
3.	Help routines	Automated procedures designed to lead the user through the process step by step.
4.	Adequate data validation	Routines designed to verify that only data meeting system specifications can be entered into the application system.

Figure 5/Operating Characteristics (cont'd)

#	EVALUATION CRITERIA	DESCRIPTION OF CRITERIA
5.	Understandable error messages	The error messages are easy to understand, explain the action taken by the application software, in what transaction or process the error occurred, and what action, if any, is required by the user.
6.	Automatic file backup description	The periodic retention of information so that in the event of a failure sufficient file information will have been retained to minimize the restart process.
7.	Report generator	The ability of the user to change the format, sequence, and content of application system reports.
8.	Integrated processing	The interconnection of two or more processes so that data generated in one process will be automatically transferred to the related process.

Figure 5/Operating Characteristics (cont'd)

#	EVALUATION CRITERIA	DESCRIPTION OF CRITERIA
9.	Adequate audit trail	The capability to reconstruct processing in the event it is necessary to substantiate or explain processing.
10.	Forgiving system	System retention of processing information so that in the event the user makes a processing error the situation is easily correctable.

that is the only item that you would select from the menu.

Usable Documentation

If you have ever stayed up into the middle of the night assembling children's toys on the evening before a holiday or birthday, you will understand what the term usable documentation means. Some believe that the people who write instructions for assembling children's toys and operating aplication software are sadists, in that they enjoy watching users become frustrated.

The characteristics of good usable documentation are:

1) Short sentences and the lack of unexplained computer jargon
2) Instructions presented in step-by-step format
3) Pictures of input/output documents with each field identified and explained
4) Illustrated examples
5) Lists of the most probable problems and what to do if they occur

Help Routines

The execution of application software is a task you will probably perform in the solitude of your own work station. This solitude may be necessary to avoid being committed for screaming a continuous string of profanities and crying when the software fails to perform as expected.

Recognizing the danger to one's mental health, some kind soul created the help routine concept. The objective of the help routine is just that -- to help you when you are in trouble.

The second law of computer science used to be "When all else fails, read the instructions." Since the advent of the help routines, that law has been changed to "When all else fails, type the word 'HELP' on the terminal keyboard." The help routines are designed to lead you through the processing in a step-by-step manner so that you can successfully perform your computer tasks. The help routines are generally of most value when you forget what steps need to be performed, the proper commands for performing the steps, or the sequence in which the steps must be performed. Help routines can also help you analyze and correct problems.

Adequate Data Validation Routines

Murphy says that whatever can go wrong in a computer system will go wrong. What Murphy didn't say, but should have said is that most of the things that can go wrong will occur when inputting data to the computer system.

The computer people have a saying for bad input, which is "GIGO" or "Garbage in - garbage out." In general, computer people believe that if you enter invalid data that it is your problem, not theirs--thus the garbage in - garbage out concept.

Data validation routines are designed to provide the highest probability that the data you enter will be correct and what you intended to enter. Some examples of data validation routines follow:

1) Numeric check - Numerical field, such as quantity ordered, telephone number, and zip code are verified to ensure that you only entered numeric data and not alphabetic or special characters.

2) Value check - The value entered in the field can be verified against a list of known values to ensure that it is correct, such as verifying that a state code entered is valid for one of the states.

3) Attribute check - An attribute of the data value is verified to ensure its reasonableness, such as ensuring that a quantity field is not greater than fifty, or that an address cannot be entered without entering a zip code.

Understandable Error Messages

One of the differences between computer processing and people processing is that the computer must predetermine what to do when an error occurs. It is not considered good practice for the computer system to be stopped while people make decisions about the type of processing that should occur. In a manual system, people can wait until a problem is encountered and then take action based upon the nature of the problem. For example, if a customer ordered a product that was temporarily out of stock, a clerk, after consultation with a supervisor, might substitute another similar product and ship the order. A computer system doesn't have that luxury. If the order is to be rejected that must be predetermined, or if a similar product is to be substituted that, too, must be predetermined.

The method of interacting with people in these problem areas is for the application software to take action and then notify the people through an error message regarding what action was taken. The normal type of computer actions are:

1) Reject the condition and notify the application users.
2) Accept the condition and issue a warning message that the accepted condition may be erroneous, such as an order for a very large quantity.
3) Take the most logical action; for example, if a quantity is not included ship a quantity of one.

The clarity of the message wording and the explanation of the message is essential to proper communication between the application software and the people using it. Well-constructed error messages exhibit the following characteristics:

- Identify the transaction and field in which the questionable event occurred.

- State in concise English the nature of the problem and action taken by the application system.

- Clearly identify what is expected of the user.

- Include in a user's reference manual a detailed explanation of each error message, together with the most probable cause of the problem and the most likely solutions.

Automatic File Backup

Computer systems use electronic recording of information, not printing on paper documents. What can be recorded electronically can be destroyed electronically. Once destroyed, there may be no way to create that data again.

Let's look at an example of Cindy creating a letter. Cindy sits at the terminal, creates and keys the letter into computer storage. During this process Cindy is using the word processing software to help format, structure, and verify spelling. Partway through the letter-writing process one of the following events occurs:

- Power interruption
- Word processing software failure
- Cindy accidentally enters the wrong command

One of the above events either electronically erases Cindy's letter, or creates a condition so that the data cannot be read. At this point, the letter is lost and Cindy must begin again to create and enter the letter. Let's assume another power interruption occurs before the letter is complete so that it is lost again and Cindy must start back at ground zero recreating and reentering the letter.

Automatic file backup is a process that periodically stores the work that is being performed on the computer onto a diskette or disk pack (a Winchester drive). If the unfavorable event should occur in a system that has automatic file backup, only a small part of the processing may be lost as opposed to the entire processing. In our example, Cindy may lose a paragraph rather than an entire letter.

Report Generator

Computer application systems record, process, and present data to the user. The software system developer must either guess in what format the user wants that data presented or offer format presentation options. A report generator is a method of providing the application software user with options on how that user would like to receive data from the software system.

The type of report options that are desirable include:

- Inclusion of report date
- Inclusion of user name or company name
- Inclusion or deletion of fields from a report
- Multiple levels of totals
- Sequencing of items in the report

This feature requires the user to do some simplified programming, but at the same time can enhance the value of information produced from the application software. The greater the report generator features, the greater the options available to the user, but at the same time, the more skilled the user must be to benefit from these features.

Integrated Processing

The computer law of data entry error states that if you enter the same piece of data twice you will make twice as many errors in entering the data. While this law is easy to understand, it may be difficult to put into practice unless the application software acquired is integrated. Let's look at a few examples of integrated software:

- Cash reciepts recorded in an accounts receivable system are automatically posted to the general ledger accounts.

- Name and address information maintained in the label file can be used in letter preparation with the word processing software.

- Items sold through an automated invoicing system are deducted from on-hand inventory.

Integrated applications provide the following three major advantages:

1) Reduced errors in data entry

2) Improved accuracy in processing

3) More timely recording of information and thus consistency between application information

Adequate Audit Trail

An audit trail is an historical record of application processing. The word audit does not mean that it is prepared for auditors but, rather, that it is prepared in order to substantiate processing. Some organizations have chosen to call this trail of processing a management trail because it is primarily needed by management.

You may need to reconstruct processing for any of the following reasons:

- Pinpoint accountability for processing

- Substantiate proof of processing for auditors for regulatory or tax agencies

- Explain to customers or involved individuals how and when processing occurred
- Reconstruct computer files in the event they are inadvertently destroyed

The information needed for audit trail or reconstruction purpose can be retained in one of the following two formats:

- Transaction processing log - A file of the transactions that have occurred and the processing on those transactions. Sometimes processing is recorded by showing permanent-type information such as an accounts receivable file immediately before and then after processing occurs.

- In-file history - The record of processing is maintained in the file itself. For example, all of the orders that a customer makes would be recorded in the customer file. Obviously, records have to be deleted eventually, but that, too, is part of the audit trail capabilities.

Some application software provides good adit trail records, and others have no audit trail at all. The two trade-offs that need to be considered with an audit trail are space requirements and cost. The more extensive the audit trail, the more costly the system and the more storage space needed to retain the audit trail.

Forgiving System

A forgiving system is one that lets you make a mistake and recoup. For example, if there are five steps in a process and you make a mistake on the fifth step a forgiving system will let you restart on the fifth step, while a nonforgiving system will make you go back to the first step and start over.

A forgiving concept is one that stores and retains adequate information so that errors can be easily corrected. Examples of some of the conditions that you would like the system to forgive you for are:

-   Making an error after performing a large number of steps correctly (you would like to restart at the point where you made an error, not the beginning of the process)

-   Inadvertently ask the system to erase information when you didn't mean to (you would like to get that information right back)

-   Erroneously change some information in a computer file (you would like to get the data back the way it was before the change)

The more forgiving the system, the easier it is to work with. Systems that are strict and hold you to the rules may take considerably more time to perform the same tasks than would be needed on a forgiving system. This is a concept which may be foreign to the noncomputer user, but anyone who has used a computer system for any length of time will clearly understand the concept and be thankful for whatever forgiveness has been built into the software system.

SATISFY REQUIREMENTS

The major purpose of acquiring software is to satisfy requirements. The vendor software support and operating characteristics deal primarily with the usability of the software. The requirement satisfaction relates to the results produced by the software. While it is possible to live with a less than perfect system from a usability perspective, it may not be acceptable to acquire software that does not produce the needed results.

The determination of software requirements involves analyzing the processing needs in order to document specifically what is wanted. However, this may be a difficult task for people who have not been trained in systems design, and in addition may not be a task that a user wants to undertake.

When one decides to acquire a home, two approaches can be taken. First the family can sit down and decide what they want and then from those desires document the requirements for their home. Using this approach, the family would have to decide on the size of the house, the location of the rooms, the height of the ceiling, etc., etc., etc. The second option is to look at the supply of available homes and determine which satisfies the housing requirement of the family or one that is close enough that with some modifications will satisfy the family needs.

This book will recommend the software requirements approach that evaluates existing software in order to find the software package that most closely satisfies your needs. Obviously, some preliminary specifications must be established just as you would if you were looking at a home. For example, you might establish that you want a four-bedroom home, not costing over $100,000. In establishing software requirements you have to have the same basic requirements before you will even consider a package. Beyond that, the best way to acquire software is

Figure 6/Satisfy Requirements

#	EVALUATION	DESCRIPTION
1.	Needed field types	The application contains all the needed information.
2.	Adequate field size	Each of the fields is of sufficient length to store all the characters or numbers needed.
3.	Needed processing capabilities	The application can perform those processes needed by the user to satisfy user requirements.
4.	Sufficient storage	The storage capacity of the computer files are large enough to retain all of the processed transaction and/or permanent data, such as names and addresses needed for processing.
5.	Ease of retrieval	The ability to retrieve a specific transaction or transactions from the file with minimal effort.

Figure 6/Satisfy Requirements (cont'd)

#	EVALUATION	DESCRIPTION
6.	Ease of use	The ability to perform the needed tasks with minimal processing and people resources.
7.	Sufficient speed	The ability to obtain the needed information from the system when it is needed by system users.
8.	Proper sequence(s)	The capability of the system data to be stored in the proper sequr resequenced if necessary to meet specific user needs.
9.	Needed reports	The application system can produce the desired information in the most appropriate format.
10.	Adequate controls	Adequate controls exist to ensure the integrity of computer processing.

to look at what is available and then make a judgment as to whether or not the software package will satisfy your processing needs.

This section will describe the general criteria by which processing needs can be evaluated. These are the general criteria that should be evaluated in any software package. However, in addition there are the business requirements that must also be evaluated and they will be discussed in a later chapter.

The evaluation criteria that can be used to determine if requirements are satisfied are listed in Figure 6 and described below:

Needed Field Types

Processing occurs on data. Only that data that is included within the application can be processed. Selected applications should contain all of the fields that are needed to perform the desired processing. For example, if an invoicing system requirement is to have both a ship to and bill to address, then the fields provided in the application software must provide for both types of addresses.

The application documentation should show examples of the input and output documents. These should be reviewed to determine whether or not the desired data exists within the application. If the needed data is unavailable, you must make a decision whether the application is acceptable without some needed data fields.

Adequate Field Size

If you have ever examined a form that prepares data for a computer system, you will notice a series of boxes. Have you ever wondered what happens if there are more letters or numbers than there are boxes? The answer is that those extra numbers or letters are lost. For example, if there are only twenty boxes to insert twenty letters for your last name, and your last name happens to be twenty-two characters long, then two of those characters are lost. If you purchase an order entry application, and the quantity field is only three characters long and your customer orders 1,002 items, the number 1,002 will not fit into three boxes. What, in effect, would happen is that the 1,000 would be lost and the order would be prepared for two items instead of 1,002 items.

As you examine applications, you should ask yourself if the field lengths are long enough for your needs. It may be necessary to do a short perusal of the data you have manually captured in the area you hope to automate so that you can estimate if the application software under evaluation has sufficient capacity in the field sizes. If not, you will have to make a decision if you can live with the smaller field sizes.

Needed Processing Capabilities

Application software is designed to perform certain types of processing. Those capabilities not incorporated into the software cannot be performed. For example, if you need to calculate both city and state sales tax, but the application does not provide for city sales tax calculations, the invoicing software will be missing a needed processing capability.

The easiest procedure to evaluate processing capabilities is to compare the input and output application documents. Processing is required to convert input data to output data. If the desired outputs are not on the output reports there is a high probability that the needed processing is not included in the application software.

Sufficient Storage

Three types of storage are needed in processing data. First is storage for the transaction data, such as manuscripts being prepared, accounts receivable, or other application data. Second is storage for permanent information, such as product prices or name and address files. Third is working storage for use during application processing. Some storage restrictions are hardware restrictions, while others are software restrictions.

It is advisable to perform a rough calculation of the three types of storage requirements. It is normally easy to determine transaction storage requirements, and permanent storage requirements. Unless some special types of processing are required, there are normally few working storage restrictions. An example might be that an invoice can contain no more than twenty line items.

Ease of Retrieval

During processing, certain information will be needed. The ease with which that information can be obtained, and whether it can be obtained, may be an important processing consideration. For example, invoices may be stored in customer number sequence or invoice number sequence, but periodically it is necessary to know how much product particular sales people sold. If the sales information is not retrievable by salespersons through normal processing it may take some abnormal and costly procedures to retrieve the desired information.

Ease of Use

The first rule of computer usage is "What is easy to use will be used." Experience has taught many users the hard way that those processes or procedures that are difficult to use are frequently not used. Obviously, this doesn't apply to the essential mainline processing, but desirable features which might be used are not used because they are difficult to use.

In later chapters we will attempt to develop selection factors, and one of these will be an ease of use factor. Knowing how easy or hard application software is to use should be one of the more important selection criteria.

Sufficient Speed

The application software must be able to produce the desired results in the required time frame. For example, if the computer was used to develop an estimate for a job, but it took several hours to develop that estimate, it may not be of much value during negotiations. It would require a break in negotiations and then a resumption if computer services are to be used. Speed should be considered in relationship to need.

Proper Sequences

People store and access data in desired sequences. For example, you may wish to access data by customer number but the application software stores sales information by invoice number. If you were to select that software and wanted information in customer number sequence, you would have to build yourself a cross-reference index so that when you wanted to acces an invoice for a particular customer you would have to look up that customer number manually to find the invoices on which they had purchased product and then access the computer file by invoice number. Having data in the sequence needed to facilitate people processing is an important selection criterion.

Needed Reports

Reports are the method by which processing results are presented to the user. The two most common methods of presenting information are screens on terminals and printed documents. The method of presenting information may not be as important as the format and content of individual reports. In a previous example we discussed the need for information by salesperson, and if such a report cannot be produced by the application software is selected without the desired reporting capability.

Adequate Controls

Controls are those collections of procedures that ensure processing is accurate and complete. Without controls, erroneous data may be accepted as correct, transactions may inadvertently be lost or added, or any number of problems can occur which will affect the integrity of the application data. Controls are the mechanisms that reduce the risk that the data produced by the computer application will be erroneous.

SOFTWARE SELECTION BY EMBARRASSMENT CHECKLIST

Selection by embarrassment is asking those questions that need to be asked to ensure that the best possible software package will be selected to meet processing requirements. The embarrassment part is when software marketing personnel cannot answer the question, or the question has detected a potential software weakness. Unfortunately, too few people ask these embarrassing questions, and then they themselves become embarrassed when they find the software package they purchased does not perform as expected.

Many purchasers of application software encounter an expectation gap. This is the gap between what they are expecting to receive and what the vendor is delivering. We encounter this frequently with many purchases that we make. For example, frequently we expect when we buy an automobile that it will be free of defects, and yet the manufacturer of that automobile only plans to control the number of defects and not eliminate them. Thus, each time a defect in our car is encountered we are disappointed because we did not expect those problems.

The expectation gap in computer software can be huge to the uninitiated. You should not expect a perfect package, but unless you do sufficient investigation by asking the proper embarrassing questions you will not understand what the software vendor expects to deliver, so you can compare that with what you are expecting to receive.

The Software Selection Checklist (Checklist #1) contains the list of embarrassing questions that you should ask during the software selection process. These are not secret questions and you may want to show this checklist to the individual offering you the software, and ask for answers to those questions.

> **SOFTWARE SELECTION SURVIVAL RULE #4**
> It is far better to embarrass the salesperson with questions they cannot properly answer than to be personally embarrassed by purchasing a useless software package.

CHECKLIST 1

CHARACTERISTICS OF SOFTWARE SELECTION CRITERIA
(A list of embarrassing questions to ask the software vendor)

#.	ITEM	RESPONSE YES	NO	COMMENTS
	Vendor Reputation			
1.	Has the vendor been in business over three years (if not, how long)?	✓		Original first to come out with micro in 1977 - Model 1
2.	Have over 500 copies of this software package been sold (if not, how many)?	✓		
3.	Can you supply me with the names of three individuals who have acquired this software package (if so, get names, addresses, and telephone numbers)?			Can't need permission

CHECKLIST 1 (cont'd)

#	ITEM	RESPONSE YES	RESPONSE NO	COMMENTS
	Software Training			
4.	Is training provided on how to use the application software (if so, what type and how much)?	✓		Complete classroom upstairs
5.	Is the training available at the time I will acquire the software package?	✓		
6.	Does the training assume that the student will possess a certain level of knowledge about the application area and data processing (if so, what kind of knowledge)?			assume no knowledge – just as far as accounting ~~package~~ goes
	Software Service			
7.	If I have difficulty working the software package, will somebody help me?	✓		
8.	If my software system fails, will I be able to get service to fix the problem?	✓		Service dept in Bangor. Bring to us or they come to you
9.	Will the service be performed in my place of business or the vendor's?	✓		

CHECKLIST 1 (cont'd)

#	ITEM	RESPONSE YES	RESPONSE NO	COMMENTS
10.	How quickly can I have software service?	✓		right away
Software Enhancements				Replace bad part — or sent in to be fixed Texas
11.	Does the vendor of this software package intend to continually improve the capabilities and qualities within the package?	✓		Constantly upgrading package Example - If tax structure changes
12.	If so, will those enhancements occur at least once per year?			
13.	Will previous purchasers of that software be able to acquire the enhanced version at a nominal price?			
Operating Characteristics				
14.	Are the processing options available in the software system presented in menu format?	✓		
15.	Is the documentation for operating the system presented in easy-to-use, step-by-step format?	✓		

CHECKLIST 1 (cont'd)

#	ITEM	RESPONSE YES	RESPONSE NO	COMMENTS
16.	Is the documentation written for someone with minimal data processing skills?		✓	
17.	Does the application software contain help routines in case I have difficulty remembering how to process a transaction?	✓		
18.	Are the data validation routines adequate to prohibit most types of improper data from entering the system (adequate should involve static checks such as numeric fields in numeric, reasonableness checks to question unusual items, and relational checks to verify cross-reference between related fields)?	✓		Vague - If type in something wrong it makes you balance it - flags you if your out of balance.
19.	Are the error messages written in concise and easy-to-understand statements?	✓		
20.	Do the error messages explain what actions the application took?	✓		In some cases can apply to more than one thing

-56-

CHECKLIST 1 (cont'd)

#	ITEM	RESPONSE YES	RESPONSE NO	COMMENTS
21.	Do the error messages state what action the user is expected to take?			
22.	Does the user manual explain the meaning of the error messages?			
23.	Does the system provide adequate automatic file backup so that recovery after a system problem will not require an exorbitant amount of reprocessing?	✓		Not automatic. Trained in making backups must put a disk in and back it up.
24.	Can the user of the application system format the report in a manner suitable to the user?	✓		Basic general format Set format — you put in accounts yourself
25.	If applications are related, such as cash receipts and accounts receivable, is data entered into one application automatically posted to related applications?	✓		Interacts
26.	Does the application software package provide an adequate audit trail to reconstruct processing?	✓		Yes, in fact. Give audit trail for previous 24 months

CHECKLIST 1 (cont'd)

#	ITEM	RESPONSE YES	RESPONSE NO	COMMENTS
27.	Does the audit trail permit tracing of transactions from the source document to the control totals to which they have been accumulated?			
28.	Does the audit trail permit identification of all the transactions that were accumulated to develop a control total?			
29.	If I make a mistake partway through processing, will the system forgive me and permit me to correct my mistake and restart at the point where I made the mistake?	✓		

Satisfy requirements

#	ITEM	RESPONSE YES	RESPONSE NO	COMMENTS
30.	Does the application software contain the data fields needed to meet the processing requirements?	✓		Certain capacity can be expanded
31.	Do the data fields contain sufficient space to include the data values that will be used during processing?	✓		

CHECKLIST 1 (cont'd)

#	ITEM	RESPONSE YES	RESPONSE NO	COMMENTS
32.	Do the output documents produce the processing results needed in this application area?			
33.	Is the storage area of permanent data large enough to meet my application requirements?	✓		
34.	Is the transaction storage space large enough to handle my volume of transactions?			
35.	Is there sufficient space in working storage to permit the type of processing needed?			
36.	Can the information included within the application system be easily retrieved?			
37.	Can the information be retrieved in the sequence in which it is needed?			
38.	Is the application easy for people to use?	✓		One of the easier to use

CHECKLIST 1 (cont'd)

#	ITEM	RESPONSE YES	RESPONSE NO	COMMENTS
39.	Can the processing results be produced in sufficient time to satisfy processing requirements?	✓		
40.	Are the files arranged in the proper sequence (the sequence I use in my business)?	✓		
41.	Does the application software produce the needed reports?			
42.	Are controls adequate to ensure accurate and complete processing?			
43.	Can I afford to purchase the application?			
44.	Can I afford to operate the application?			

3
THE SOFTWARE SELECTION PROCESS

*Rarely does good software come looking for you—
you must look to find it.*

Tom needed a word processing software package for writing letters to customers. Off he marched to the computer store to select the needed package. "Hi," said the computer store merchant, "what can I do for you today?" Tom explained what he wanted to do and the merchant quickly responded, "I have just the package you need." The merchant led Tom to a computer, inserted a diskette, and showed Tom how easy it was to write a letter. "Look at this," said the merchant, "if I don't want this word I simply move the cursor, hit a couple of buttons, type in a new word, and the line immediately adjusts." Tom paid the $300, took a diskette and an instruction manual, and left the store, whistling.

Once home, Tom's world began to fall apart. First he found he didn't have enough storage in main memory to even run the package. That could be solved for another couple of hundred dollars. Then Tom found the letter file couldn't be merged with the name and address file, meaning he would have to enter the name and address each time he wanted to write a letter, even though the objective of the package was to produce several hundred of the same letter. Next, Tom found that while the words in a sentence closed up when a correction was made, it would leave gaps in the paragraph which looked unsightly. The net result—Tom still has his letters typed manually.

I wish I could tell you this was an isolated story, but it's not. The computer is still the black box. The computer people are still the high priests and priestesses of our technological society. How dare we, the computer novice, question the computer store priests and priestesses? We need a software selection process that is easy to use which does not consume more than a couple of hours per software package. This chapter presents the solution to software selection.

WHAT DO THEY KNOW IN THE COMPUTER STORE?

An important question for the prospective purchaser of software is: "How much does the person selling me software know about the computer?" This may seem to be a funny question to ask, but ask yourself how much do I expect the individual pumping gas into my car to know about the functioning of an automobile. In answering that question, you would probably say to yourself if that individual knew a lot about the functioning of an automobile they wouldn't be pumping gas.

Some people in the computer store may be very knowledgeable, but others are not. If you know the computer business you can tell the two apart. If you don't know the computer business you might be easily fooled.

Let's look at what you can reasonably expect from the individual selling you software, which is to:

    o   Know the names of the software packages available for sale

- o   Know the cost of the software package
- o   Use some technical jargon (which they probably like to use)
- o   Recognize that their salary is based on their ability to sell software
- o   Respond, "No problem" when asked how difficult anything is.

Remember that many computer stores are franchises. The franchisor explains in a one-week course to the franchisee all they need to know about the computer business. By the time you have read and digested this entire book you may know more about computer software and its attributes than the individual selling you the software. The rule of thumb in the data processing profession is that it takes two years of full-time experience to become qualified in programming, and five years of experience to be fully qualified to design computer systems. How much experience and knowledge did you say that salesperson had?

SOFTWARE SELECTION SURVIVAL RULE #5

If the person selling you software is inexperienced, they can't help you, they can only tell you the facts. If you don't ask the right questions, you won't know the right facts.

WHAT DO YOU NEED TO KNOW BEFORE YOU SELECT SOFTWARE

Chapter 2 has explained in detail the characteristics of a good software package. It is basically the answers to the forty-four embarrassing questions from Checklist #1 that you need to know prior to selecting software.

The following five items represent the information that you should obtain prior to acquiring a software package:

1) Does the software package satisfy my processing requirements?
2) Is the software package easy to use?
3) How will I learn how to implement and use the software package?
4) What type of support will I receive if I have problems?
5) What does the software package cost?

Once you have the answers to these five items you will know whether or not to acquire the software package. The remainder of the book is designed to explain how to answer those questions.

THE WHY, WHO, WHEN, WHERE, WHAT, AND HOW OF SOFTWARE SELECTION

Most software will be purchased in a computer store. Software can be ordered through the mail but that option should be reserved until you have a better understanding of software and the selection process. In other words, don't buy your first few packages through the mail.

The software selection process, as with any other acquisition process, is a three-part process. The first part is the need definition, the second part is fact finding, and the third part is decision making.

Most application software sells in the range of $100-500. It is in the dollar range that most people can afford, and thus I might ask why I should spend several hours of my life selecting something that may only cost $100 or $200. If we want a new suit, don't we just go to the clothing store, look at what they have, decide if it's what we want, and buy it? Why should we not do the same process for computer software?

The cost of acquiring software is only part of the software cost, while the cost of the suit is the total cost of the suit. The software cost that is not built into the price tag is:

- o   Cost of learning the software
- o   Cost of performing functions that the software doesn't do-- but should
- o   Aspirins or other libations taken to relieve the frustration caused by software problems

The proposed software selection process is a five-step process which explains what should be done in selecting software. However, prior to describing the five-step process let's describe why we go through a selection process, who should do it, when it should be done, where it should be done, what should be done, and then the five-step how-to-do-it process.

Why A Detailed Selection Process?

There are two options available in acquiring software. Under the first and least desirable option you are sold software. This is what happened to Tom in his acquisition of a word processing software package. The second and desirable option is that you buy the software. However, you can only buy software when you understand the product that you are buying. Thus, the need for a detailed, methodical selection process.

Who Should Select the Software?

If it is your computer, and you are the only one involved in operating the computer, skip to the next section, because you are the one who is going to do the selecting. On the other hand, if there are several people involved the individual doing the selecting should be the one who will operate the software package. That is the individual who has to live with it, work with it, and make it work. This doesn't preclude several people from being involved in the selection process but, rather, ensures that the user of the software is not excluded from the selection process.

When Should Software Be Selected?

Allowing yourself sufficient time to look and evaluate avoids the pressure of having to acquire the package the first day you begin looking. A three-month lead time would be an ideal selection period. The three months would provide you time to research, inquire, study, examine, and make a decision. Less than a one-month lead time is generally undesirable, especially until you become more experienced in the process.

Many mistakenly believe that software can be acquired, brought home, plugged in, and it will work. This may happen, but it is normally the exception rather than the rule. This doesn't mean that the first day you won't be able to do something with the software; what it means is that by the time you have been trained, entered needed information, such as names and addresses, and gained sufficient confidence that you know what you are doing, a few days or even weeks may have passed.

> **SOFTWARE SELECTION SURVIVAL RULE #6**
> Begin the software selection process one to three months prior to when you need the software operational.

Where Should the Selection Process Occur?

Industrial psychologists discuss a theory called "turf theory." The theory says that when you are on your own turf you are in a dominant position, and when you are on another person's turf they are in a dominant position. This means that if the selection process occurs on other than your turf you will not be in charge of the process. If it occurs on your turf you will be in charge.

Let's look at the three parts of the selection process and then decide on whose turf that part of the process should occur. In the first part you are establishing your requirements. This should occur on your turf, your place of business, or where you will be doing the computer processing. The second part of the selection process is fact finding. Since you need information and the computer store has that information, you have no option but to visit their turf to identify the facts. Since this is the noncritical part of the selection process, little will be lost by having this occur on the other person's turf. The last part, the selection decision, is the most critical part of the selection process and should occur at a location where you are under the least pressure. Making a no decision is a high-pressure decision in the computer store, but can become a very logical, rational decision when it occurs on your own turf.

What Are the Selection Methods, Tools, and Techniques?

The individual selecting software is cautioned against becoming overly impressed by the technical aspects of the selection process. If you were selecting an automobile and concentrated on the functioning of the differential, the gear ratios, carburetor performance, and combustion pressure, the process would seem overwhelming. On the other hand, if your concerns were with miles per gallon, manufacturer's guarantees, roominess of the automobile and number of doors, the process of selecting a very complex piece of machinery becomes doable.

The methods, tools, and techniques used in the selection process must be ones that are readily understandable and easy to use. A sampling of the selection tools and techniques that will be covered in this book are:

- Kick-the-tire test - The survival rules of thumb presented in this book that formalize the experiences of many, and present them in an easy-to-use, intuitive format.

- Demonstrations - Touching, feeling, using, and observing the performance of the software on a computer.

- Q's and A's - A list of embarrassing questions to ask during the selection process, with guidance provided on the type of answers that are most desirable to the questions.

- Comparison shopping - A formal method of rating the attributes of two or more similar software packages in order to arrive at a quantitative number to help you decide which is the best software package for you.

- Show and tell - A process in which you develop some general requirements for the software package and then either show or tell those requirements to the computer store personnel in order to determine if a specific package meets your basic requirements.

How To Conduct the Selection Process

The selection of software is a new process for many people. Therefore, the selection process will be presented in a step-by-step format. This is designed to simplify the process, and at the same time explain the order in which the selection steps should be performed.

Each of the five selection steps will be described in detail in Chapters 4 through 8. The chapters will contain the tools, techniques, checklists, and survival rules needed in the performance of that step. Following these steps will put you in the driver's seat of the selection process.

OVERVIEW OF THE FIVE-STEP SELECTION PROCESS

The five-step software selection process is outlined in Figure 7 and described below:

Step 1 - Define Requirements

The selection process begins by identifying and describing processing needs. The recognition that a need exists may occur in one of two ways. First, a process or task is very time-consuming and help is sought in performing the task. In this approach, there is a need in search of a solution. The other approach is an awareness that a specific software package exists. For example, the awareness that a word processing software package is available to help in letter or report writing. In this instance, there is a solution available to satisfy a need if it exists. Without this step you may find yourself in the position of buying a highly skilled tool for which you have no need.

Figure 7/Software Selection Steps

STEP #	STEP NAME	DESCRIPTION
1.	Define Requirements	The task to be performed by the software, plus the methods by which those tasks should be performed if appropriate.
2.	Establish Selection Criteria	Assigning priorities to the requirements as a basis for evaluating available software. The prioritization can be as simple as required and optional, or requirements can be listed in the sequence of importance.
3.	Identify Software Alternatives	Locating the software packages that should be considered in the software selection process.
4.	Compare Software Packages	An orderly process of showing the relationship between the common processing characteristic of two or more software packages.

Figure 7/Software Selection Steps (cont'd)

STEP #	STEP NAME	DESCRIPTION
5.	Select the Software Solution	A formal process of allocating points to the software packages being considered based upon the ability of those packages to satisfy the selection requirements. The software package receiving the maximum number of selection points becomes the software solution.

Step 2 - Establish Selection Criteria

When purchasing software it is unrealistic to expect a perfect fit any more than you can hope to find the perfect house or perfect automobile. In order to ensure the best possible fit, the requirements should be prioritized so that the selector will be sure that the software package satisfies at least the high-priority requirements.

Step 3 - Identify Software Alternatives

The process of finding a solution for processing requirements is to identify the contenders. If the processing problem is common, such as word processing, there will probably be many solutions, each of which emphasizes specific processing features. On the other hand, if the software needed is highly specialized, such as a lens design program, then there may only be one option available. However, this doesn't mean that it will be easy to find that single package.

Step 4 - Compare Software Contenders

Two methods are used in selecting software. One is to use intuition and judgment to select a package. The other is to compare the characteristics of two or more software solutions so that a decision can be made on a more scientific basis. This step explains how to document software characteristics so that they can be used in the decision process.

Step 5 - Select the Software Solution

This step proposes the scoring method to determine which software package should be selected. The selection criteria attributes will be assigned a weighted value and each software package under consideration will be allocated a given number of points based on how well that package satisfies the evaluation criteria. The software package getting the greatest number of points represents the software package that should be selected.

> **SOFTWARE SELECTION SURVIVAL RULE #7**
> The time spent on a methodical software selection process is minimal compared to the time spent trying to make the wrong software work.

4
STEP 1—DEFINE REQUIREMENTS

He who knows what he wants has a much greater chance of finding it than he who doesn't.

THE EASE OF MISINTERPRETING REQUIREMENTS

A popular party game begins when a story is written on a piece of paper. The story is secretly communicated to the first individual, who must then orally relate the story to the second individual. The second individual then orally relates the story to the third individual, and so on, until it has been passed on to the last individual in a chain of story tellers. This individual then tells the story as they heard it to the entire group. At this point, the story on the piece of paper is reread to the group, usually among great laughter. Often there is little relationship between what the last individual stated to be the story and what it actually was.

The definition and explanation of requirements between the individuals needing the software and the individual having the software to sell may result in a miniature version of the story-telling party game. What the customer, which is you, tells the salesperson are your requirements are interpreted and misunderstood by that individual. Again, remember that neither you nor the salesperson may have had much data processing experience. Thus, while you may appear to be communicating, the actual technical messages sent and received are in different languages, and no communication is occurring.

One of the classical cartoons of the data processing profession is illustrated in Figure 8. This shows how the requirements to build a simple swing are misinterpreted, misunderstood, and misdirected in building the swing for the user. Documenting requirements in the format suggested in this chapter can help eliminate many of those communication problems.

THE COMMUNICATION CHALLENGE

One of the great challenges in any technology is the ability to communicate needs into technical requirements. We recognize the difficulty we have explaining to children concepts such as love, fear, and hate. These challenges multiply as we grow and attempt to comprehend that the world is round, that ice cream is made up of atoms, and that there is really music in a record.

Computer technology is equally as mystifying as the fact that television can be transmitted through the airwaves. How, then, are we going to communicate our needs and requirements into a language that is understandable by the technicians? If we fail to do this properly we may be disappointed in the product we buy.

This chapter attempts to bridge the technological gap between the nontechnical person with a processing requirement and the technical world of EDP. The chapter is designed to help you speak computerese

Figure 8/Misinterpreted Requirements

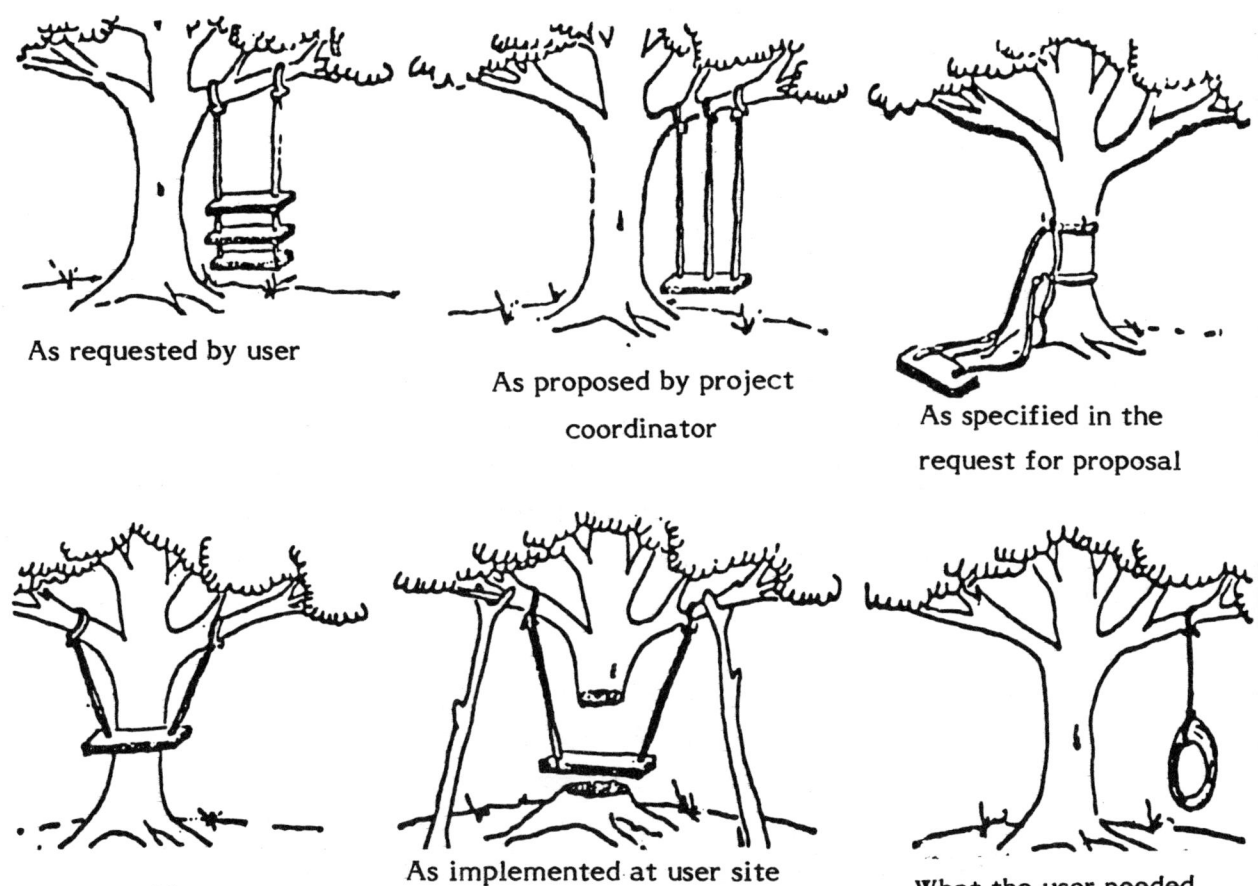

fluently enough to have your needs satisfied. The chapter will even include a little computer jargon in case you want to impress your friends.

THE TOTAL SYSTEM CONCEPT

The computer technician has yet to recognize that people are an essential ingredient in the performance of a processing task. Most computer technicians hope that people will go away and frequently build their system on the premise that people are unimportant and may, in fact, go away.

On the other hand, it's people that make any computer system work. A concept exploited by the computer technician is that computers don't make mistakes, people do. What the computer technician often overlooks is that the failure to recognize people is the cause of most of the mistakes.

For example, improper instructions lead to mistakes; difficult-to-use forms lead to mistakes; poorly designed reports lead to mistakes.

> **SOFTWARE SELECTION SURVIVAL RULE #8**
> Good computer software recognizes the importance
> of people in processing, while poor computer
> software only tolerates people.

The total system concept recognizes that processing begins and ends with people. People originate transactions that require processing, and use the results of processing as a tool in completing their processing tasks.

The total system concept is illustrated in Figure 9. This illustration shows that people originate data using manual techniques. The information is then entered into the computer, processed, and outputs prepared. At the conclusion of computer processing, the results are used by people in their day-to-day work.

Let's look at an example of a financial inventory forecast. One of the more popular software packages for the personal computer is VISICAL. This package will create a financial model for an individual such as an inventory requirements forecast. To use the VISICAL program the user must originate data which in this example would be sales forecasts. This is performed manually. The individual then enters that data into the computer and it is processed using the VISICAL software to produce a sales forecast and inventory requirements list. This is all performed by the computer. The output report showing the inventory requirements is then used by the individual as a basis for ordering product. The purchase order in our example is prepared manually. Thus, the individual originated the data that is used in processing, operated the computer program, and also used the results. Who said that people aren't important in computer processing?

THE ORIGIN OF DEFINING REQUIREMENTS

Who makes up the processing requirements? We have identified that you, the customer, are responsible for the requirements because you

Figure 9/Total System Concept

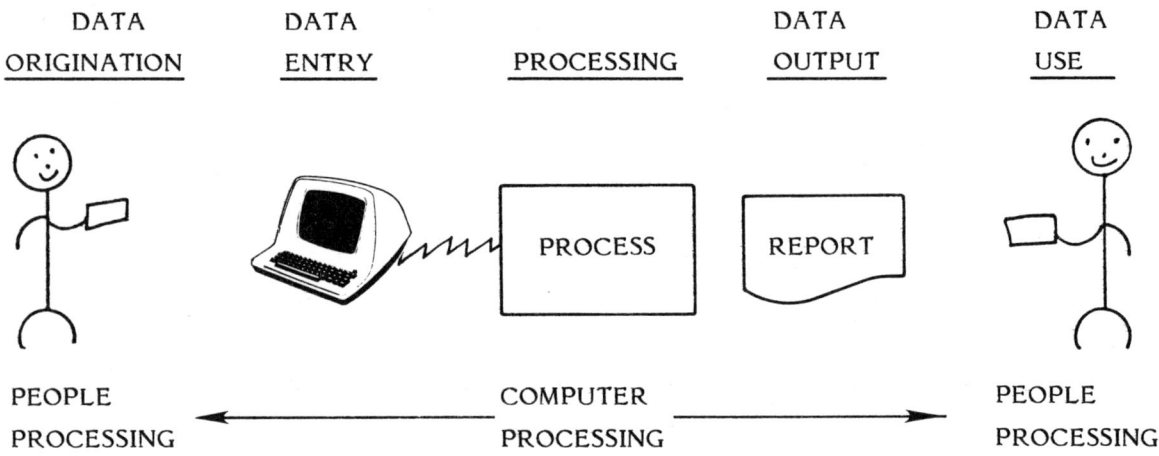

are buying the product. On the other hand, you may not know enough about computer processing to be able to write a decent set of processing requirements. In addition, some people may not know what they want until they see it. A meal can sound scrumptious on a menu, but the moment it is delivered to your table you know you don't want it.

One of the first requirement decisions that you must make is "Should this processing task be performed on the computer?" If you can answer any two or more of the following questions yes, then the tasks should be considered for computer processing:

SHOULD THIS TASK BE AUTOMATED QUESTIONNAIRE

		RESPONSE
AUTOMATED CRITERIA QUESTION		YES NO

1. Is this task performed in the same manner at least once per week?

2. Does the task require over four hours of people effort per month to perform?

3. Does the task require information to be acquired from a file or catalog of over fifty items?

4. Are three or more mathematical calculations performed in processing a transaction?

5. Is the number of errors made in processing this area manually unacceptable?

6. Are more than ten of the same type transactions processed at the same time?

If the computer is to be considered for this process, then there are two methods of defining processing requirements. First, you can sit down and list the requirements as you perceive them for processing. Second, and perhaps the more common approach, is to examine one or more existing software packages for the process you want to accomplish, and draw out of those packages your set of requirements.

The origin of defining software package requirements is illustrated in Figure 10. This shows the two alternative approaches. In one the requirements are known, but the software available to satisfy those requirement is unknown. In this instance you document your list of requirements and then go search for software. In the second alternative, the software is known but your requirements are unknown. In this instance you go to the computer store and study or observe a demon-

Figure 10/Origin Of Defining Requirements

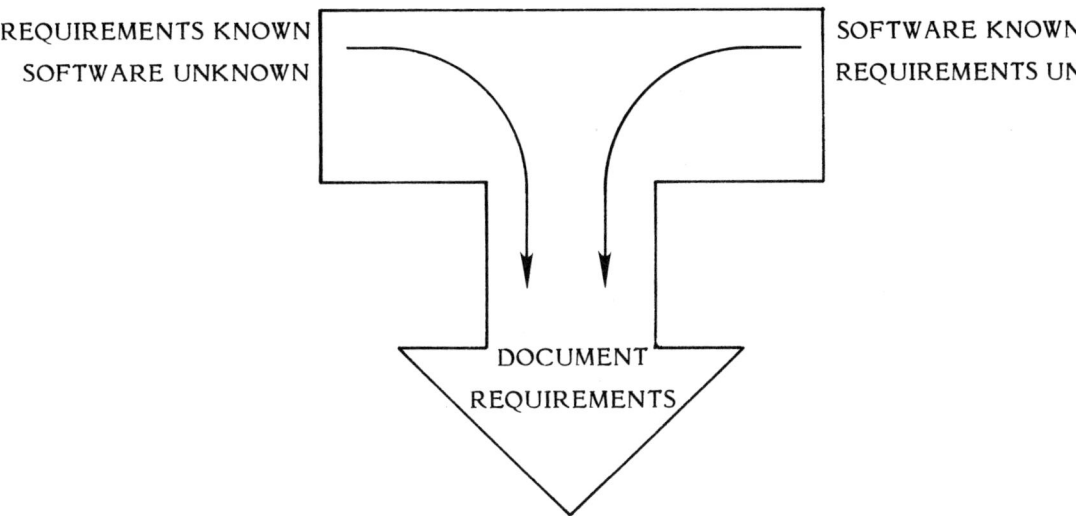

1. Fields needed

2. Field size

3. Processing

4. Storage

5. Ease of retrieval

6. Ease of use

7. Speed of processing

8. File sequence

9. Reports

10. Controls

stration of the available software, and from that document your requirements.

The latter method is the recommended method for the computer novice. It is the equivalent of knowing that you want an automobile but aren't sure what kind you want until you visit the showrooms and see what is available. After looking in three or four showrooms your requirements begin to become firm, and the selection process takes on a semblance of order. When you have limited EDP skills, and knowledge of what applications can and can't do, this not only helps in the selection process but is also an educational experience in the operation of a computer.

> SOFTWARE SELECTION SURVIVAL RULE #9
> One of the cheapest and potentially best sources of computer education is competitive shopping for application software

The requirements for application software are the same as the characteristics discussed in Chapter 2 to satisfy requirements. The ten criteria that satisfy processing requirements and are to be used in specifying requirements are listed at the bottom of Figure 10.

WHAT KIND OF APPLICATION SOFTWARE IS AVAILABLE?

The type and variety of application software available is almost unlimited, and is growing every day. While it is not beyond reason for computer users to develop their own software, with few exceptions it is probably not necessary.

The most popular categories of application software are:

- o   Financial accounting software - The basic accounting record keeping performed by businesses including invoicing, payroll, inventory control, preparation of financial statements, and tax accounting.

- o   Financial modeling - The ability to perform a variety of financial modeling and analysis often used in the business planning process. This software is commonly called VISICALC, although it is also sold under other trade names.

- o   Word processing - Software that can organize, structure, correct, and merge data into letters, reports, and other documents. A valuable feature of many word processing programs is a dictionary of 10,000 or more words, including terms entered by the user, to check spelling.

- o   Games - Fun and pleasure programs having the objectives of both teaching how to use the computer and just having a good time.

A listing of the common types of application software is included in Figure 11. This listing is far from exhaustive, but does provide a sample of the more popular application software. In addition, many

Figure 11/Common Types of Application Software

ACCOUNTING

Account Keeper
Accounting Plus II
Accounting Plus II Biz
  Package
Accounts Receivable
Accounts Receivable Balance
  Forward
Accounts Receivable/Sales
  Analysis
ACS Basic Accounting System
AMI Client Write-Up
Asset Record System
B/F Accounts Receivable
  System
Billings Management
Bookkeeper II General Ledger
Bookkeeper II-Depreciation
BPI General Ledger
Business Accounting
Business Check Register and
  Budget
Business Control System
CPA

ACCOUNTING (cont'd)

Client Accounting System
Construction Accounting
CPA Client Write-Up
Datawrite Client Write-Up
  System
Delivery Service Automation
Depreciation Calculations
  and Reports
Executive Accounting
  System
Financial and Management
  Accounting
Financial Partner
Fixed Asset Accounting
Fixed Asset Depreciation
Fixed Assets/Depreciation
  Schedules
Fund Accounting System
General Accounting
General Accounting Package
General Ledger
Glector
    Insoft Accountant System

Figure 11/Common Types of Application Software
(continued)

ACCOUNTING (cont'd)

Integrated Accounting System
IRAP
Ledger System Business Module
Management - Financial
  Reporting
MAXILEDGER
Microaccountant Accounting
  System
MICROLEDGER
MJA Multi-Journal Accounting
Nominal Ledger
One-Type Accounting System I
One-Type Payroll and
  Accounting
Paysystem Accountant
Peachtree General Ledger
SBCS General Ledger
SNIP - Integrated Accounting
TCS Accounting
TCS Client Ledger
TCS General Ledger
TCS Total Ledger

ACCOUNTING (cont'd)

The Accountant Finance
  Data Base
The Bookkeeper System
The Boss Financial
  Accounting
The Business Bookkeeping
  System
The Controller
The Depreciation Planner
The Software Fitness
  Program

AGRICULTURE

Adjusted Weaning Weights
BEEFUP-Herd Management
  Performance
Cattle Feeding Economics
Corn Harvest Losses
Corn vs. an Alternate Crop
Cow-Calf Profitability
Crop Yields

Figure 11/Common Types of Application Software
(continued)

AGRICULTURE (cont'd)

Economics of Corn Production
Farm Management
Farrow-To-Finish Swine
  Production
Feeder Pig Production
Fertilizer Formulation
Field Population
Field Size
Finishing Feeder Pigs
Job Cost (Crop Cost)
Least Cost Fertilizer
  Application
Liming Soil
Liquid Manure and Fertilizer
Net Energy for Feedlot Cattle
PEDIGREE-5 Generation
  Annotated Pedigree
Protein Balancing for Feedlot
  Cattle
SBCS Agri-Ledger
Selling Wet Corn vs. Dry
Sheep Production Economics

AGRICULTURE (cont'd)

Soil Erosion
Soybean Harvest Losses
Swine Ration Analysis
Swine Ration Formulation

APPLICATION PROGRAM DEVELOPMENT AIDS

A-FORTH
ABT Pascal Tools
APEX-6502 Assembly
  Language
Apple-80 Disassembler
Assembly Language
  Development System
AUDEX-Audio Programming
  Aid
CBASIC Program
  Maintenance Utilities
CINDEX
Cosapple 1802 Disassembler

Figure 11/Common Types of Application Software
(continued)

APPLICATION PROGRAM DEVELOPMENT AIDS (cont'd)

CRTFORM Programmer Productivity
Diagnostics II
DISTEL-Disk Based Disassembler
Executive Planning System
Floating Point Dictionary
Forms 2
Key-Perfect-Checksum Table Generator
Linkdisk-Disk Utility for Apple Pascal
Linkvideo-Screen Utility
Lower Case Character Generator
MULISP/MUSTAR-80
OGI-Forth-Implementation of FIG-Forth
Pascal Programmer
Pascal Level 1

APPLICATION PROGRAM DEVELOPMENT AIDS (cont'd)

Pearl III-Rapid Logic Generator
Personal Programmer
Prism/Ads Data Base Generator
Program Development System I
Program Writer for Non-Programmers
Programming Aids 3.3
Quic-N-Easy Application Development
RAID-Real Time Assembly Debugger
Scientific Data Base
SID-Symbolic Instruction Debugger
Stok Pilot-Menu Generator
STRING-80

Figure 11/Common Types of Application Software
(continued)

APPLICATION PROGRAM DEVELOPMENT AIDS (cont'd)

STRING-BIT
Systems-Analyst
Teacher Plus Teaching & Reference Pkg
The BASIC Teacher
The Last One-Program Generator Pkg
The Toolbox Programming Utilities
Tiny-C Interactive Programming
UCSD Pascal
Unlock Development Tool
V-COM Disassembler Package
Z8000 Cross Assembler

BUSINESS MANAGEMENT TOOLS

Analyst-Business Productivity
Apple Sack General Business Program

BUSINESS MANAGEMENT TOOLS (cont'd)

Bookkeeper II-Sales Analysis
Business Pac 100
Business Planner
Creative Financial Package
Desktop/Plan
Execuplan Planning & Forecast
Financial Modeling System
Financial Planning Series
Financial Planning/Analysis
Finplan/Financial Planning
FP2020 Financial Planner
FPL-Financial Planning Language
Magic Worksheet
Magicalc-Forecasting Package
Micro-DSS/Finance

Figure 11/Common Types of Application Software
(continued)

BUSINESS MANAGEMENT TOOLS (cont'd)

Microfinesse-Financial Modeling
Milestone-Critical Path Network Analysis
Optimiser
PFS-Personal Filing System
Personal Report System
Plan 80-Financial Planning & Analysis
Project Boss-Mgr's Cost Control System
Project Planning and Budgeting
Retail Purchasing & Pricing
Salary Planner
Senior Analyst
Supercalc-Electronic Spread Sheet
Support Pkg for Real Estate Mgmt

BUSINESS MANAGEMENT TOOLS (cont'd)

T/Maker II-Visual Calculating Tool
The Analyzer
The Budget Planner
Universal Business Machine Planning and Forecasting
VisiCalc III
VisiCalc Real Estate Template

CAPITAL PROJECTS PLANNING & CONTROL

Angle Project Scheduling
APM-Project Management System
Jobtrak-Project Tracking
Milestone Project Management
Project Management System

Figure 11/Common Types of Application Software
(continued)

CAPITAL PROJECTS PLANNING & CONTROL (cont'd)

Project Planning

COMMUNICATIONS

Apple Access III
BISYNC-80
BSTAM
Class Data Recorder
CM-900 Burroughs Network Services
Communications Program
Crosstalk Smart Terminal/ File Transfer
Data Capture 4.0
Data Transporter Package
Datalink
DTS-3-Serial Data Transfer
Electronic Mail
IBM-CP/M Allows Transfer of Data

COMMUNICATIONS (cont'd)

IE/Modem
Intercom Communications
METTY-Intelligent Terminal Package
Micro-Courier
Micro-Telegram
Microlink-80-File Transfer
Reformatter-CP/M-IBM Data Transfer
Remote Console Program
Smarterm-CP/M Terminal Program
Term II-Computer Intercommunications
Term Intercommunications Package
TTY-Communications With Other Computers
U-Net-Shared Resources Network

Figure 11/Common Types of Application Software
(continued)

COMMUNICATIONS (cont'd)

Ultimate Transfer
Visiterm-Communications
  Package
VT-100 Emulator
Western Union Interface

DATA MANAGEMENT

ANALYST
CBS-Configurable Business
  System
CCA Data Mgt System
CM 2020 Configurable Manager
Condor Series 20
Data Management Program
Data Manager
Data Master
Data-View Electronic Filing
  Cabinet
Database II
Database Management

DATA MANAGEMENT
(cont'd)

Datafax
Dataflow-Info Processing
Datastar
Datastore
Datatree
Disk-Edit-Screen Oriented
  Disk Editor
DMS-Data Mgmt System
FABS II-Rapid Keyed Access
Fast Entry for Tabs Business
  Modules
FINDAFYL-Reference
  Retrieval System
FMS 80-Data Base
  Management System
GBS Database
General Database
HDBS-Hierarchical Data
  Base
IFO Database Manager
Information File Organizer

Figure 11/Common Types of Application Software
(continued)

DATA MANAGEMENT
(cont'd)

Information Master-Data Mgmt
  System
KTDS-Key to Disk, Data Entry
Linkindex-Pascal Utility
MAG/Base-Data Base Management
Manager-Relational Data Base
MDBS DRS-Micro Database
  Mgt System
MUMPS-Language for CP/M
  Database
Optimum Data Mgmt Program
PRISM/IMS-Information Mgt
  System
RADAR-Random Access Data
  Acquisition
Reprogrammable Data Base
Scientist-Data Base &
  Statistical Pkg
Selector III-Data Base
  Processor
Selector IV-Data Base Mgt

DATA MANAGEMENT
(cont'd)

Selector IV-Key Access Info
Selector V-Data Base Mgmt
STATPRD-Integrated
  Database System
Stoneware Utility Package
Super Kram II - Multi-keyed
  Random Access
The Reprogrammable Data
  Base Program
VisiDex-Data Base Mgt
  System
VisiFile-Data Base Mgt
  Package
Whatsit? Conversational
  Query/Retrieval

DATA SECURITY SYSTEMS

Absolute Security
Encode/Decode Security
  System

Figure 11/Common Types of Application Software
(continued)

DISTRIBUTION

ABT Retail Manager
Beer Distributor Management
Inventory, Order Entry,
 Invoicing
Oil Jobber Management System
Order Entry and Inventory
 Control
The Store Manager
Wholesale/Retail Distribution
 System

EDUCATION - BUSINESS

Accounting Tutor
Comparative Buying
Income Meets Expenses
Interactive Typing Tutor
Job Readiness-Assessment
 & Development
Master-type-Typing
 Instruction

**EDUCATION - BUSINESS
(cont'd)**

Money Mgmt Assessment
Typing
Typing Tutor
You Can Bank On It -
 Bank Concepts

**EDUCATION - CHEM/
PHYSICS**

Acid-Based Chemistry
Atomic Structure
Chem Lab Simulation
Chemical Equilibrium
Chemistry With A Computer
Fundamental Skills for
 General Chemistry
High School Chemistry
High School/Jr. College
 C.A.I. Biology
High School/Jr. College
 C.A.I. Physics

Figure 11/Common Types of Application Software
(continued)

EDUCATION - CHEM/ PHYSICS (cont'd)

Organic Nomenclature
Physics

EDUCATION - ENGLISH

A Batch of Endings
Agreement of Pronoun/ Antecedent
Alphabetize
Capitalization
Catalog Cards
Commas
Compu-Read
Compu-Spell
Coordination
End Marks
Excess Words
Faulty Coordination
Hearing the Homonyms
Irregular Verbs
Is It "ie or ei?"

EDUCATION - ENGLISH (cont'd)

Language Drill
Locate Books on the Shelf
Magic Spells
Misplaced Modifiers
Parallel Structure
Possessing the Possessives
Prefixes & Suffixes
Quotations
Reading Level
Readings in Literature
Run On Sentences
Scramble
Sentence Diagramming
Sentence Fragments
Speedreader
Spell-N-Time
Spelling Bee with Reading Primer
Spelling Those Plurals
Still More Nasty Demons
Subject/Verb Agreement

Figure 11/Common Types of Application Software
(continued)

EDUCATION - ENGLISH (cont'd)

Subordination
The End of the Endings
Those Nasty Demons
Understand the Card Catalog
Understand the Title Page
Use an Index
Use the Table of Contents
Using Adjectives/Adverbs
　Correctly
Word Scrambler & Super
　Speller

EDUCATION - MATH

Addition & Subtraction
Algebra I
Basic Math Skills
Compu Math: Arithmetic
　Skills
Compu-Math Decimals
Compu-Math Fractions

EDUCATION - MATH (cont'd)

Counting Bee
Decimal Estimation
Division Drill
Drill II
Elementary Math
Fractions
Geometry
Geometry and Measurement
　Drill
Lessons in Algebra
Matching and Using Numbers
Matching Geometric Figures
Math-Addition & Subtraction
Matrix Mathematics
　Package
Measurements
Multiplication & Division
Mumath-PO Symbolic Math
New Subtraction
Numerical Analysis
　Mathematics

-97-

Figure 11/Common Types of Application Software
(continued)

EDUCATION MATH
(cont'd)

Problem Solving
Problem Solving in Everyday
  Math
Sets
Sign Drill/Typing
Statistical Analysis I
  Mathematics
Statistics 3.0
Typing Fractions

EDUCATION - MISC.

2ES Courseware
American History Through
  Biographies
American Indians
Antonyms
Apple Sack 2 Home Education
Approximate Measure
Astronomy I & II
Concentration-Taxing

EDUCATION - MISC.
(cont'd)

Counting Calories
Early Civilization
Educational Package
Educator's Disk
Family Fun
Farm and Farm Products
HI-Res Life
History
Home Safe Home
Insects
Light Pen Quiz
Literature
Living Things
Math, Sports, Etc.
Middle Ages
Money
Moptown
Mother Goose Rhymes
Music/Art
Our Bodies
Poison Proof Your Home

Figure 11/Common Types of Application Software
(continued)

EDUCATION – MISC.
(cont'd)

Questions & Answers in
  Biology
Questions & Answers in
  History
Quizstat
Reverse/Sampling
School Days
Sentence Beginning
Shore Features
Sound
Supermap
Synonyms
Systems of the Body
Teacher Create Series
Teacher Plus
Telling Time
The Basic Teacher Pac
The Earth and It's
  Composition
The Professional-Teaching
  Program

EDUCATION – MISC.
(cont'd)

The Solar System
Transportation History
Typing
United States
Visual Perception Tests
Weather Fronts
Work Relationships
World Desert Region
World Polar Regions

FINANCE-INVESTMENT &
PORTFOLIO ANALYSIS

Analysis 1-Stock Trend Data
  Analysis
Commoapx System
Computicker
Computrac File Reader
Dow Jones News & Quotes
  Reporter

Figure 11/Common Types of Application Software
(continued)

FINANCE-INVESTMENT &
PORTFOLIO ANALYSIS
(cont'd)

Dow Jones Portfolio Evaluator
Dowlog-MC
Electronic Stock Package
Engineer's System For Trading
Forecast I
Forecast II
Fotofolio-Visual Display
  w/Statistics
Gann's Square of Nine
  Analysis
Intelligent Investor
Investment Analysis
Market Charter-Technical
  Analysis
Moneybee-Investment Analyst
Options 80-Stock Options
  Analyzer
Portfolio Master
Quotecharter
Quoteprocessor

FINANCE-INVESTMENT &
PORTFOLIO ANALYSIS
(cont'd)

Ratortn-Investment Analysis
Stock and Options Analysis
Stock Forecasting
Stock Market Management
Stock Market Utility
Stock Option Analysis
Stock Tracker
Stock Valuation Program
Stocksheets
Strategy M-Monitor Price
  Change Dynamics
The Clover Method Trading
  System
The Stock Portfolio Program
Tickertec-Tickertape
  Program
Wilers 6 Systems Analysis

Figure 11/Common Types of Application Software
(continued)

FOREIGN LANGUAGES

Chinese Lessons
Foreign Words and Phrases
Greek Roots and Prefixes
Japanese Lessons
Latin Roots and Prefixes
The French Hangman
The Russian Disk
The Spanish Hangman

GAMES

Adventures
Alien Rain
Alien Typhoon
Almanac - The Time Machine
Amaze
Analiza
Animal
Anti-Ballistic Missile
Apple Adventure
Apple Bowl
Apple Fun

GAMES (cont'd)

Apple Panic
Apple Sack 3 - Adventure
  Pak
Apple Sack 7 - Space Sack
Apple Sack 8 - Game Sack
Apple Sack 9 - Base Star
Apple Stellar Invaders
Apple-oids
Asteron
Astro-Scope
Astrology
Autobahn
Backgammon 20
Battle of Midway
Beer Run
Best of Muse
Biorythms
Blackjack
Both Barrels
Brands
Bridge 2.0
Bridge Tutor

Figure 11/Common Types of Application Software
(continued)

GAMES (cont'd)

Bubbles, Planetoids and Burnout
Cartels and Cuthroats
Castle Wolfenstein
Chambers of Xenobia
Chebychev 1
Chebychev 2
Chronicles of Osgroth
Civil War
Compu-Math Arithmetic
Compu-Math Decimals
Compu-Math Fractions
Computer Air Combat
Computer Baseball
Computer Bismark
Computer Conflict
Computer Napoleonics
Computer Quarterback
Cops and Robbers
Cosmo Mission
County Carnival
Cyber Strike

GAMES (cont'd)

Disk Talker
Dr. Chips
Dragon Fire
Dungeon
Executive Fitness
Falcons
Fantasyland 204
Fastgammon
Fight Simulator
Galactic Attack
Galactic Wars
Galaxy Wars
Games People Play
Gamma Goblins
Bobbler
Golf/Cross-Out
Gorgon
Hammurabi
Head On Game
Hellfire Warrior
Hi-Res Football
Hi-Res Soccer

Figure 11/Common Types of Application Software
(continued)

GAMES (cont'd)

In The Army Now
Into Ships
Jet Fighter Pilot
Klondike 2000
Lost By Ship
Mastermind
Meteoroids in Space
Micro Othello
Mimic
Mind Games Package
Mission Asteroids
Mystery House
Need an Analyst
Nominoes Jigsaw
Oil Tycoon
Olympic Decathlon
Operation Apocalypse
Orbitron
Outpost
Paddle Fun
Pegasus II

GAMES (cont'd)

Perception 3.0
Phantoms Five
Planetoids
Plot 3D
Pokeno
Poker Slot Machine
Pool 1.5
Pot'O Gold I
Pot'O Gold II
President Elect
Pro Football
Pro Picks
Project Omega
Pulsar II
Race for Midnight
Raster Blaster
Red Baron
Rendezvous
Robot Wars
Sahara Warriors
Sargon II (Chess)

Figure 11/Common Types of Application Software
(continued)

GAMES (cont'd)

Satellite Trak
Shell Games
Shuffleboard
Skybombers
Skybombers II
Sneakers
Snoggle
Soft Porn
Softside Publications
Space Eggs
Space Warrior
Spellguard
Spelling Bee
Star Cruiser
Star Dance
Star Thief
Startraders
Startrek
Stock
Sub Attack
Tawala's Last Redoubt
Teacher's Pet

GAMES (cont'd)

Temple of Apshal
Terrorist
Tetrad
The Strip
The Asteroid Field
The Great Escape
The Horse Selector II
The Prisoner
The Scorekeeper
The Shattered Alliance
The Warp Factor
Three Mile Island
Torpedo Fire
Ultima
Voyage of the Valkyne
War and Games
War Games
Warp Factor
Watch Your Moves
Win at the Races
World's Greatest
    Blackjack

Figure 11/Common Types of Application Software
(continued)

GAMES (cont'd)

Wumpus
Xplode

**GRAPICS/COMPUTER-
 AIDED DESIGN**

3-D Surface Plotter Package
A2-3D1 Graphics Family
ABT Barwand Software
Action Sounds & Hi-Res
 Scrolling
Apple Plot
AppleGraphics II
Artist Designer
Bar Chart (Histogram)
 Graphics
Business Graphics III
Circuit Designer Graphics
Circuit Simulator
Creativity Tool Box
CURVFIT
Data Plot

**GRAPHICS/COMPUTER-
 AIDED DESIGN (cont'd)**

E-Z DRAW
FLGDZINE
Graforth - Development
 Tool
Graph-Fit
Graph-Pak
GRAPHPOWER
Hi-Res Secrets
Line Graphics
MC Painting
ORIFICE
Pascal Animation Tools
Pascal Graphics Editor
Perspective Plot - 3-D
 Graphics
PGE - Graphics Editing
 Package
PILOT-Animation Toolkit
Polar Coordinate Plot
RGL Real Time Graphic
 System

Figure 11/Common Types of Application Software
(continued)

GRAPHICS/COMPUTER-AIDED DESIGN (cont'd)

Screen Director
Shape Table Generator
Stats-graph
Super Shape Draw & Animate
Tablet Graphics
The Coloring Board Program
The Designer
Topographic Mapping
Ultra Plot
Utopia Graphics Tablet
  System
VACVESL - Vacuum Vessel
  Design
VESDZINE - Design of
  Vessels
VISITREND/VISIPLOT
X-Y Vector Plot Package

HOME MANAGEMENT

Address File

HOME MANAGEMENT (cont'd)

Auto Records
Checkbook Balancing
Checking Account
  Management
Chequemate
Diet Analysis
Financial Analyzer
Five Minute Financial
  Check-Up
Grocery List
Home Finance
Home Inventory File
Home Money Minder
Home Purchase Analysis
Magazine File
Mortgage Analysis
Personal Accounting System I
Personal Expense Record
Personal Finance Manager
Personal Financial Planning
Programmed Exercise

Figure 11/Common Types of Application Software
(continued)

HOME MANAGEMENT (cont'd)

The Personal Check Manager

INCOME TAX

Dow Jones Portfolio
 Evaluator
Individual Tax Planner
Micro-Tax Individual Tax
 Package
Micro-Tax Integrated
 State Income Tax
Micro-Tax Partnership
 Package
SHORTAX - Tax Planning
 Package
Tax Planner
Tax Preparer
TRPS - Tax Return
 Preparation System

INVENTORY CONTROL

ARM1000 - Rental Business
Basic Business Inventory
Bill of Materials
BPI Inventory Control
Intotory Inventory System
Inventory Accounting
Inventory Control
Inventory Management
Inventory Management
 for Stock Control
Inventory Pac
Inventory System Business
 Module
Manufacturing Inventory
 Control
MATSTAT-Materials
 Tracking
Order Entry/Inventory
 Control
Peachtree Inventory System
Point-Of-Sale Retail System

Figure 11/Common Types of Application Software
(continued)

INVENTORY CONTROL (cont'd)	JOB & CONTRACT COST ACCOUNTING
Property Manager for Moveable Equipment	Billflow
Retail Inventory	Bookkeeper II-Job Costing
Rogis Stock Control for Components	BPI Job Costing
Stock Control	Contract Billing
Stock Recording	Contractor Job Cost
Stockfile Inventory System	Cost Accountant
Stockroom Inventory and Purchasing	Job Accounting System
	Job Control System
Structured Systems Inventory Control	Job Cost Accounting
	Project Cost Accounting for Architects
TCS Inventory Management	
The Order Scheduler	Project Cost Accounting for Engineers
	The Software Fitness Job Cost Analyst
	Time Recording-Job Cost Analyst
	Timerec-Transaction Carry Forward

Figure 11/Common Types of Application Software
(continued)

MAILING LIST & LABEL PROCESSING

Address Book Mailing List
Apple-III Mail List Manager
Apple Mail Sack
Apple Post
Benchmark Mail List
Commercial Mailer
Mail List
Mail80 Mailing List
 Software
MAILER-Name & Address
 Management System
Mailing Address
Mailing List Package
Mailing System
MAILMERGE
MAILPRO
Mailroom-Mailing List
 Management
Master Mailing List
NAD-Name & Address
 Selection System

MAILING LIST & LABEL PROCESSING (cont'd)

Name and Address
Postmaster-Mail Management
Professional Mailout
School Mailer
Small Business Mailing &
 Filing
Super-M-List Mailing List
 Program
Ultra Plot/Mailing &
 Filing System I

MARKETING/SALES ANALYSIS

EASYTRAK-Salesmen Monitoring
 Package
Marketing Systems - Proposal
 Developer
Office and Agent
 Productivity Package
Sales Analysis

Figure 11/Common Types of Application Software
(continued)

MARKETING/SALES ANALYSIS (cont'd)

Sales Pro Prospect Mgt
 Package
Sales Tracker
SALESLOG - Sales Mgt
 Program
SNAP - Questionnaire
 Design and Printing
TCD Life Insurance
 Computer System

MISCELLANEOUS

BILL - Building Energy Use
Circuit Analysis
Hand Holding BASIC
Insulate
Mini-Warehouse System
Stepwise Multiple
 Regression

MUSIC

Alpha Syntauri Music
 Synthesizer
Apple Music Theory
Apple Sack Music &
 Graphics
Appleodion Music Synthesis
 System
Music System
Musicomp
The Electric Duet

ORDER ENTRY/ACCOUNTS RECEIVABLE

BPI Accounts Receivable
 Program
Cash Receipts System
Company Sales
Invoice Compiler
Invoicing
Membership Billing
MICROREC

Figure 11/Common Types of Application Software
(continued)

ORDER ENTRY/ACCOUNTS RECEIVABLE (cont'd)

Multi-Property Accounts Receivable
Open Item Accounts Receivable
Order Entry
Order Entry and Billing
Order Entry and Invoicing
Order Tracking System
Peachtree Accounts Receivable
Peachtree Sales Invoicing
Progressive Billing
Purchase Order System
Receivables Systems Business Module
Receiver
Sales Invoicing
Sales Ledger
Sales Order Processing

ORDER ENTRY/ACCOUNTS RECEIVABLE (cont'd)

Software Fitness Program - A/R System
Structured Systems Accounts Receivable
T-SOP Sales Order Processing
TCS Accounts Receivable Package
TCS Total Receivables
The Biller

PAYROLL PROCESSING

Advanced Payroll Package
After-The-Fact-Payroll - updates records
Apple Payroll System
Bookkeeper II-Payroll
BPI Payroll
Business Basic Payroll System

Figure 11/Common Types of Application Software
(continued)

PAYROLL PROCESSING (cont'd)

Contractor Payroll
Jobcost Payroll
Micropayroll
Passive Payroll
Paymaster
Paymaster-Payroll System
Payrecord I
Payroll
Payroll Accounting Package
Payroll Assistant
Payroll I
PeachPay
Piece Rate Payroll System
Post Facto Payroll
Print/Paycheck Accounting
　System
Run Tme Payroll Program
Sheltered Workshop Reporting
Structured Systems Group
　Payroll
TCS Payroll Package

PAYROLL PROCESSING (cont'd)

TCS Total Payroll
Variable Workers'
　Compensation
WH-347-Accessory program
　for Jobcost

PERSONNEL MANAGEMENT

AMI Post-Facto Payroll
MICROPERS - Payroll &
　Personnel Mgmt
Personnel Data Recorder
Personnel Office -
　Federal Compliance
Personnel Record
Personnel Record/Employee
　Records System

Figure 11/Common Types of Application Software
(continued)

PROFESSIONAL OFFICE SYSTEMS

AMI Omegabyte Time & Billing
BETA - Stand Alone Time &
  Billing System
Billkeeper - Professional
  Billing
Client Billing System
Client Record/Bill
  Preparation
Datalaw System 3-Law
  Office Mgmt
DataTime
Dental 80A-Dental Acctg
  & Billing
Dental Billing Package
Dental Office Management
DentalEase
Dentistaid - Dentist
  Office Management
Insyst (Insurance System)
Legal Billing & Timekeeping
  System

PROFESSIONAL OFFICE SYSTEMS (cont'd)

Legal Clerk - Office
  Management System
Legal Time Accounting
  System
Medicaid Day Treatment
Medical Accounting and
  Billing
Medical Clinic
Medical II - Office Mgmt
  System
Medical Office Management
Medical Secretary
Medical/Dental Management
  System
Medical/Manager
MedicalEase
MedPak
Medtips - Billing &
  Insurance Forms
PAS - 3-Patient Billing
  & Accts Receivable

Figure 11/Common Types of Application Software
(continued)

PROFESSIONAL OFFICE SYSTEMS (cont'd)

Patient Accounting System
PIP-Payroll/Invoicing
 Program
Professional Office
 Management
Professional Time &
 Billing
PTA - Professional Time
 Accounting Pkg
Series 8000 Dental Mgmt
Series 8000 Medical Mgmt
Series 9000 Family Dental
 Management
The Patient Scheduler
Timeclok
Timemaster - Time
 Accounting
Timesaver Client Billing
 System

PROGRAMMING LANGUAGES

Ada Compiler
APL/V80 Language
Apple III Business Basic
Apple III Pascal
Apple FORTRAN
Apple Logo
Apple PILOT
ASM 65-Assembler
BASIC A+ - Extended
 Business Basic
BASIC Compiler
BASIC-80
BASIC/Z - Native Code
 Compiler
BD Software "C" Compiler
C Compiler
CBASIC 2 Compiler
CIS COBOL
COBOL 80
Cos Assembler
Cos COBOL

Figure 11/Common Types of Application Software
(continued)

PROGRAMMING LANGUAGES
(cont'd)

Focal 65-High Level
 Programming
Forth 86
Forth-Language Compiler
FORTRAN 80
FORTRAN IV
Hand Holding BASIC
KBASIC - Microsoft Disk
 Extended BASIC
Language System with
 Apple Pascal
LISP-80 Compiler
MAC 8080 Macro Assembler
MULISP Compiler
MULISP/MUSTAR 80
muMath/muSim 80-High Level
 Programming
Nevada COBOL Compiler
Pascal Compiler
Pascal/M86

PROGRAMMING LANGUAGES
(cont'd)

Pascal/MY+With SPP-ISO
 Standard
PL/1-80-Programming
 Language
RATFOR - FORTRAN
 Language
S-BASIC
SSS FORTRAN Compiler
Softronics
Stiff Upper Lisp
TCL Disk BASIC
 Interpreter
TCL-Pascal
TEC 65-Editing Language
Tiny BASIC High-Level
 Language
Tiny C
Tiny Pascal
Tiny-C-Two Compiler
Transforth II
UCSD Pascal

Figure 11/Common Types of Application Software
(continued)

PROGRAMMING LANGUAGES (cont'd)

Whitesmith's Compiler
XPLO-Structured Language
XY BASIC Interactive Process Control

PROGRAMMING UTILITIES

Apple Sak 4 - Utility Package
Basic Utility Disk
Disk Utilities 3
Disk Utility Package
Disk-o-Tape-Pascal
DOS Tool Kit
File Maintenance Package
MAG/Sam Keyed File Mgmt System
MAG/Sort-Record Sort
Masterdisk-disk Sector Editor
MSORT - for COBOL 80

PROGRAMMING UTILITIES (cont'd)

Pascal Utility Library
Pascal - Sort Program
PSORT - Pascal File Sorting
QSORT - Sort/Merge Program
SORT/B - Hybrid Sort
Supersort
Ultrasort

PURCHASING/ACCOUNTS PAYABLE

Accounting Payable
Accounts Payable Business Module
Accounts Payable/Purchase Order
Bookkeeper II - Accounts Payable
Cash Disbursements Posting System

Figure 11/Common Types of Application Software
(continued)

PURCHASING/ACCOUNTS PAYABLE (cont'd)

Check Writer
Company Purchases
Contractor Accounts
  Payable
Disk-O-Check
Micropay-Accounts
  Payable
Print Check Accounting
  System
Purchase Ledger
Structured Systems Group
  Accts Payable
T-POP - Purchase Order
  Processing

REAL ESTATE

American Software Property
  Management
Apartment Building Investment
  Analysis

REAL ESTATE (cont'd)

Apartment Manager
Commercial Property System
Construction Cost/Profit
  Analysis
Cornwall Apartment
  Management
Income Property Analysis
Listings
Multi-Property Accounting
  System
Office/Apartment Real
  Estate Management
Property Analysis System
Property Management
Property Management System
Property Mgmt - G/L Tenant
  and Expenses
Real Estate Analysis Program
Real Estate Analyzer
Realty Package
Rent vs. Buy
Rental Manager

- 117 -

Figure 11/Common Types of Application Software
(continued)

REAL ESTATE (cont'd)

Residential Property
  Management
Tax Deferred Exchange Model
Tenant Processing Package
The Landlord-Property
  Mgmt System
VisiCalc Real Estate
  Templates

TIME MANAGEMENT
& SCHEDULING

Agenda Files
APM - Project Scheduling
Appointment Calendar
Color Calendar Package
Datebook Appointment
  Calendar
Datebook Time Management
  System
GUARDIAN - Computerized
  Scheduling

TIME MANAGEMENT
& SCHEDULING (cont'd)

Office Manager - Staff
  Appointments
Personal Datebook
Professional Secretary
PROSCHED - Project
  Schedule
Time Manager

WORD PROCESSING

Apple World Oriented Text
  Editor
Apple Writer II
Apple Writer III
Benchmark - Word Processing
  System
Docuwriter Text Processor
Easywriter Word Processing
EDITRIX 1.0 - Word
  Processing
Form Letter Module

Figure 11/Common Types of Application Software
(continued)

WORD PROCESSING (cont'd)

Formulex - Business Form
  Design
Goodspell
Letter Master - Basic Word
  Processor
Letteright Correspondence
  Processing
Letterite Word Processing
  System
Magic Spell - 20,000 Word
  Dictionary
Magic Wand - Phrase
  Insertion
Magic Wand - Word Processor
Magic Wand - Word Processing
  System
Magic Window Word Processor
MAIL-MERGE-Wordstar
  Enhancement
Manuscripter - Word
  Processor
Master Text Processor

WORD PROCESSING (cont'd)

Memorite III Word Processing
Microspell Spelling
  Corrector
PALANTIR - Word Processing
  and Accounting
Personal Text Processing
Report Writer - Word
  Processing
Script III
Secretary - Word Processing
Spellbinder Word Processing
Spellguard
Super-Text Word Processing
Supertext II
TEXTWRITER III - Text
  Formatting Program
The Word Spelling Checker
VTS-80 CP/M Word Processing
WordIndex
WordMaster - Comprehensive
  Editor

Figure 11/Common Types of Application Software
(continued)

WORD PROCESSING (cont'd)

Word Master Text Editor
Word Star - Word Processing

software packages not included on the list are developed for special-interest groups or purposes such as motel reservations, dental billing, etc.

CAN I CONSIDER ANY AVAILABLE SOFTWARE PACKAGE FOR MY COMPUTER?

Unfortunately, software packages are designed to run on specific computers, or computers developed using the same computer architecture. Before you purchase any software package, verify that it can run on your computer.

A preferred method of entry into the computer field is to acquire the software that you need first, and the hardware second. Unfortunately, many people use exactly the opposite approach, which immediately places restrictions on the software you can select.

The following are the four major restrictions that need to be considered in evaluating whether a specific software package can run on your computer:

Restriction #1 - Hardware Architecture

The hardware vendor may include or eliminate processing instructions or capabilities that prohibit a software package from executing. For example, some architecture is eight bit and other, sixteen bit. The developer of software always indicates on what hardware the software can operate.

Restriction #2 - Main Memory Size

Application software is a program which will require a predetermined amount of storage of main memory storage to operate. You may not purchase as much main memory storage as is needed to execute some hardware packages. For example, you may buy a computer with 32K of main memory, but the software package you want may require 64K of main memory in order to operate.

Restriction #3 - Input/Output Devices

Application software makes use of input/output devices during processing. If your computer does not have the minimum input/output device configuration, you may not be able to effectively execute some software packages. For example, if a printer is required, and your computer does not have a printer, you may not be able to produce some or all of the reports created by the application software.

Restriction #4 - Operating System

The operating system is that piece of software which performs most of the mechanical functions during computer processing. Application programs are written to interface with specific operating systems. You may have the proper computer hardware, memory size, and input/output devices needed to operate the software but if the application software cannnot interface with your operating system it cannot execute. One of the most common operating systems is CP/M. This operating system is used on the computers manufactured by many different vendors and thus, because of the large number of potential users, is an operating system that many software vendors write for.

> **SOFTWARE SELECTION SURVIVAL RULE #10**
> Application software satisfies your needs. The hardware and operating system are the vehicle necessary to operate your application software. Therefore, the most satisfactory computer selection approach is to select the software first and then find the best hardware on which to operate your application software.

DOCUMENTING APPLICATION SOFTWARE REQUIREMENTS

A few months ago, I received an invoice from a department store for zero dollars and zero cents ($0.00). I thought to myself that the department store must be doing well financially if they could afford to send me invoices for zero cents and then promptly threw the statement away. The next month, much to my surprise, I received another invoice from the same department store for the same amount, but this time marked that it was thirty days overdue and they would appreciate prompt payment. What a joke, I thought, how could I be overdue for $0.00, and again I laughingly threw the statement into the trash can.

The next month the intensity of the message increased, this time threatening to cancel my credit with the store if I failed to pay the

$0.00 within ten days. This has got to be a joke, I thought, and again threw it away. The next month I got a letter, obviously computer prepared, from the department store's legal department threatening to take me to court unless I immediately paid the $0.00. "Enough is enough," I screamed, and I immediately sat down and wrote the department store a check for $0.00. Obviously, the department store computer was pleased, because by return mail I got a thank-you letter for paying my account in full.

The moral of this story is that the computer will do whatever it is instructed. The action does not have to make sense to the computer; all it must do is follow instructions precisely. Thus, it becomes important for the user of application software to understand what the computer is going to do, because whatever it is instructed to do, it will.

The difference between people and computers can be demonstrated by explaining how each might be instructed and execute the instructions to drive an automobile to work. The route is determined and both the individual and the computer are given directions on which routes to take to get to work. The person gets in the car and begins following the route, when he discovers a bridge has been closed for repairs. The driver immediately says, "Aha, I must take a different route," and proceeds to cross the next bridge and arrives at work only a few minutes late. That same morning the computer gets in the car and also finds that the bridge has been closed for repairs. However, the computer will do exactly as instructed, and it has been instructed to cross that bridge. Although the repairs will take eighteen months, the computer will sit and wait until the bridge is repaired and then, following the instructions, cross that bridge and get to work eighteen months late.

The documenting of requirements and evaluating software packages against those requirements will not provide complete assurance that the computer will not wait eighteen months to cross the bridge. The software package may contain several thousand instructions, making it impossible for you to guarantee prior to use that there are no flaws in the software. For example, no matter how much evaluation you do prior to purchasing an automobile it is no guarantee that the machine will work flawlessly.

What defining software requirements will do is increase the probability that you will be satisfied with the software you acquire. For most users, this exercise can be completed in less than an hour and frequently within a few minutes. If done prior to examining software, hand it to the salesperson. I can guarantee they will be impressed, and the amount of time and attention given you will increase significantly.

SOFTWARE SELECTION SURVIVAL RULE #11
Computer stores are filled with window shoppers who are greeted courteously but no real effort is made to help them. The knowledgeable shopper, the one that can present documented software requirements, will be separated from the crowd, possibly assigned the better salespeople, and treated as King Customer with all the due time, attention, and respect needed.

A form for documenting application requirements is presented as Figure 12. This "Show and Tell" Requirements Worksheet provides a quick method for describing what you expect a software package to accomplish. The form includes space for documenting the ten requirements characteristics of good application software.

A brief explanation follows on how to complete the form:

1) Fields needed - Indicate the data that you need processed by the application software. You should describe the data in enough detail to ensure your requirements are met. For example, it may only be necessary to state that you need a name and address, and that could be considered a field, but for an invoicing system if it is important that you differentiate city, county, and state sales tax then you may want to list those as three separate fields. If more fields are needed than spaces provided on the form, attach a separate sheet.

2) Minimum field size - The data value for any field cannot exceed the maximum space allocated for that field. For example, if five positions are allowed for zip code that is fine in the United States, but if you mail to Canada they have a six-position mail code which would not fit into the five-position zip code. It is these little details that cause the computer to sit and wait eighteen months for a bridge to be repaired or to mail invoices for $0.00.

Figure 12/"Show and Tell" Requirements Worksheet

Data requirements:

1. Fields needed	2. Minimum field size

3. Processing requirements:

    a) _____
    b) _____
    c) _____
    d) _____

4. Storage requirements - number of:

    a) Transaction records: _____
    b) Master records: _____
    c) Internal processing: _____

Figure 12/"Show and Tell" Requirements Worksheet (cont'd)

5. Ease of use requirements (check all which are appropriate):

   ☐ no EDP skills   ☐ no application skills   ☐ no concentration skills

6. Need to retrieve:

   a) _____
   b) _____
   c) _____

7. Transaction processing should be completed:

   ☐ in less than 1 second
   ☐ in less than 10 seconds
   ☐ in less than 1 minute
   ☐ in less than 10 minutes
   ☐ in less than 1 hour
   ☐ in less than 1 day

8. File should be in sequence on: _____

9. Reports wanted: Fields in report:

   a) _____   1) _____
                                        2) _____
                                        3) _____

Figure 12/"Show and Tell" Requirements Worksheet (cont'd)

                                                                             4) _____

                                                                             5) _____

                                                                             6) _____

b) _____ 1) _____

                                                                             2) _____

                                                                             3) _____

                                                                             4) _____

                                                                             5) _____

                                                                             6) _____

c) _____ 1) _____

                                                                             2) _____

                                                                             3) _____

                                                                             4) _____

                                                                             5) _____

                                                                             6) _____

10. Application should be controlled on (check all appropriate):

☐ field _____ (totaled)
☐ data validation
☐ transaction counts
☐ other (specify)_____

3) Processing requirements - Describe in general terms the type of processing desired. For example in a word processing program you may want a dictionary to check spelling, a global search capability to locate and change all of the same words or phrases; for example, if you had misspelled a person's name a global search would identify everywhere that name was used and then correct it to the proper spelling. Again, the processing requirements need be no more detailed than is necessary to explain what you hope to accomplish. On the other hand, don't err on the side of too little detail, because computers are detailed and either do or don't do processing actions.

4) Storage requirements - Indicate the storage requirements in terms of the number of transactions you expect to process in a given time frame such as month; the number of master records that you need to store at any one point in time such as customer name and address records; and any internal processing needs such as processing an invoice with up to twenty line items. If there are more than one type of transaction, master record, or internal processing requirements, please list them all.

5) Ease of use requirements - Ease of use is a difficult characteristic to measure. The suggested method to indicate this is to identify the skills that are not needed to operate the software. The easiest systems to use are those that do not require EDP skills, application skills other than to know how

to interface with the application, and concentration skills. In other words, if the individual has to devote their full time and attention in order to make the system work, it is not an easy system.

6) Need to retrieve - Indicate the information that you will want to retrieve from the application system, such as a customer's account balance or letters stored in a file.

7) Processing time frame - Indicate the amount of time in which you would like processing to occur. The form provides for a series of options ranging from one second to unimportant. Generally, where time is unimportant processing is dependent upon people, such as when using a word processing program.

8) File sequence - Indicate the field on which you would like the file or files to be in sequence. For example, you may want a payroll file to be in sequence by payroll number and an accounts receivable file in sequence by customer number.

9) Reports wanted - Indicate the specific reports that you want, and the data that should be contained in each report. A report can be something prepared on the printer, or isplayed on the computer terminal screen. Generally, the documented reports should be those which are essential to the success of the application.

10) Application controls - Indicate how you want the application data to be controlled. Generally, this will be the same method as used in the manual processing for this application. For example, if you control accounts receivable by totaling customer balance you would expect the application software to control on the same field. This may be a difficult category to complete without some computer knowledge, but establishing some minimal levels of control and determining that the application software provides those minimal levels is also indicative that control has been considered in the development of the application. Be wary of a financial application in which you cannot find out information on how it is controlled.

This form can be fully completed before you go to look at and evaluate software, or you may wish to wait until you have looked at some software before you complete it. If completed partially or fully before you begin looking at software, give the form to the salesperson as a basis for discussion about the software. If you haven't completed the form, give a blank copy of this form to the salesperson and tell them that you will need to obtain this type of information about the application you are evaluating before you will make a decision on whether or not to purchase that software.

Be aware that this process will scare the uninformed software salesperson. It is much easier to talk in generalities than specifics. If you are unable to get this information about the software you are evaluating, beware—unless you are the type that enjoys blind dates, purchasing surprise packages, and mystery outings.

> **SOFTWARE SELECTION SURVIVAL RULE #12**
> If the computer salesperson doesn't know but thinks it might, the software probably doesn't do what you are inquiring about.

5
STEP 2—ESTABLISH SELECTION CRITERIA

A product selected by emotion will be unsatisfactory if emotions change.

One of the great mysteries in life is how people select the products that they purchase. Advertising agencies have been attempting to unlock that age-old mystery for centuries. The ad agency attempts to identify the criteria that people use for buying a product, and then exploit that in their advertising.

Let's look at some of the criteria used by the developers of computer software to sell their product:

1) Easy to use - Vendors know that people are apprehensive about a computer and therefore want to convince them that this software package can be successfully used by kindergarten students who can neither read nor type. The objective is valid, and if you purchase the software package for this reason I sincerely hope it is easy to use. On the other hand, what is the basis for deciding it is easy to use? Is it easy for the manufacturer to use, or is it easy for you to use? What is meant by the word easy? We previously described some of the desirable concepts of easy, meaning no EDP skills, no application skills, and minimal concentration when using the software. Is this what the vendor means by easy?

2) Fast - The software can do in minutes what it would take people days to do. Again, a very desirable trait if the thing that can be done in minutes instead of days is what you want done. On the other hand, what you want done might take hours instead of minutes to do if you use the computer. Everything is not quicker to do on the computer than it is to do manually. Before you buy on the speed of the computer, be sure that the tasks that it performs quickly are the tasks you want performed, and know how long it is taking you to perform those tasks so you know what the potential savings might be. For example, a task that takes you four hours to do and can be done in four minutes on the computer sounds great until you realize that you only do the task once per year.

3) Instant information - You may see an ad showing an executive at a desk with a terminal on the side of the desk displaying the latest information. Again, this represents the power of the computer, but is it the power that you want? How do you run your business or perform your job? Do you need the instant information; would it be helpful; or would it be confusing?

When you are examining software, you will be bombarded with these advertising claims. The claims will be in ads, on the package containing the software, and in the instruction book. The salespeople may not know much about the product but they do know a lot about the advertising claims. You may hear how fast the product is, how quickly you can get certain types of information, and how easy it is to use.

When you hear or read the advertising claims for a piece of software, keep the following questions foremost in your mind:

1) Is the advertised feature an important part of the software application area, or is it just advertising hype? For example, in a general ledger system it is not important to have immediate access to the financial information contained in that system.

2) Is that feature needed by me in my job?

3) If the feature is needed, how important is it to me in selecting a software package?

The objective of establishing selection criteria is to put you in control of the selection process. If you know what you want, and how important each of those wants are, then you will select the best possible package for your needs. On the other hand, if you haven't firmly established what you want, and the importance of each of those wants, you may be talked into buying a software package that is not the best possible package to satisfy your requirements.

SOFTWARE SELECTION SURVIVAL RULE #13

You can only select the software you want when you define the criteria for selection prior to selecting software.

SELECTION CRITERIA CATEGORIES

The criteria to be used in selecting software are the criteria that are important to the user. The following five categories encompass the most common criteria:

- o   Restrictions
- o   Support
- o   Operations
- o   Requirements
- o   Cost

The restrictions have been discussed in Chapter 4 and the support, operations, and requirements criteria in Chapter 2. These become the basis for establishing the final selection criteria.

Cost can be a confusing criterion to evaluate in the software selection process. The cost to purchase software is easy to identify and evaluate. What is difficult to assess is the total acquisition cost, and the cost to operate the software.

The same cost considerations are involved in the purchase of an automobile. After you have looked at a car you know the list price of the automobile and, perhaps, the price the dealer will sell it to you for. This is the equivalent of the list price of the software. Now you must determine what other costs are involved in the purchase of the automobile, which might be:

- License plates
- Freight from factory to the dealership
- Local preparation costs
- Sales tax

Once these items have been added to the list price of the automobile, the total cost to acquire the automobile is known. In the acquisition of computer software the purchase price may not be the only cost of the software. The other costs that you need to consider are described later in this chapter.

Once you acquire possession of a product such as an automobile the expenses of operating the car begin. The automotive expenses include gasoline, oil, repairs, insurance, new license plates, and personal convenience items such as seat covers. Experience shows that the cost of operating an automobile in a few years exceeds the purchase price of an automobile. The same analogy holds true for computer software.

The cost of operating a computer includes many hard-to-quantify costs. In addition, users of application software may not have a means for recording or pricing their own time, and may not consider their personal time a cost of operating software any more than they would the personal time they expend washing their automobile. However, if the acquisition of software is to be approached from a business perspective then all of the costs involved should be considered.

The more common costs involved in operating software can be categorized into tangible and intangible costs as follows:

o   Tangible software operating costs

- Printer forms (prorated for usage)
- Diskettes (prorated for usage)
- Employee salary and benefits (prorated for usage) if any
- Equipment depreciation/rental (prorated for usage)
- Equipment maintenance (prorated for usage)
- Training costs

o   Intangible software operating costs

- Personal time
- Space/electricity/air conditioning
- Resources spent correcting problems incurred through software problems or misuse
- Poor decisions/loss of time or customer business attributable to inaccurate or untimely computer data

It would take an accountant to perform a detailed cost calculation as described above. On the other hand, it only takes some common sense to realize that special forms or large amounts of personal or employee time involved in the use of software cost money. The suggested method is to write down on a list all of the out-of-pocket acquisition costs, and a ball-park estimate of the operation costs. If this is done for each of the software packages, it will be easy to approximate the cost involved in the acquisition and operation of a software package.

An example of the type of cost lists that might be prepared for the acquisition of a word processor software package is illustrated in Figure 13. This illustration shows that when the needed components and taxes are added to the purchase price it increases from $400 to $517.95. If another word processor were to include the dictionary option, the instruction manual, and diskette as part of the purchase price, you could pay $500 for that word processor and the prices would be approximately the same.

The operation costs in Figure 13 are the costs to be considered when evaluating the cost of executing the word processor. The operation costs listed are not the people time because information would be recorded on the typewriter if the word processor wasn't used, and thus the people cost would be about the same. Also, there may be very little difference in people cost from word processor to word processor from an entry perspective, and thus the cost is not of value in comparing different word processor software packages or the use of a word processor versus the typewriter.

The operation costs that are listed are those that would be helpful in comparing word processor packages. For example, the dictionary spelling check for the X Star word processor being evaluated takes four minutes per page to perform. If another word processor could do it in two minutes it may be a cost factor that could decide which word

Figure 13/Software Cost List Example

Software Package: "X" Star Word Processor

Acquisition costs:

Purchase price	$400.00
Tax	20.00
Diskette	5.00
Instruction manual	17.95
Dictionary option	75.00
TOTAL COST	$517.95

Operation costs:

Dictionary spelling check	- Four minutes per page
Automatic backup	- Every page
No global search	- Average three of this type error per document so must correct each individually without the global search feature

processor to select. The automatic backup performed on every page may reduce the operating cost in the event problems occur; and the fact there is no global search means, as indicated on the software cost list example, that the individual would have to manually correct three of this type of error per document. Again, if another software package had a global search option the value of that option can now be estimated.

SETTING SELECTION PRIORITIES

We all recognize the need to establish priorities in life, but few of us are disciplined enough to carry out the concept in practice. Why, then, if we select jobs, buy homes, marry a spouse, and make other important decisions without going through this priority-setting exercise should we do it for software selection? The answer is that you may not need to if you have been happy with all of your other selections.

The purpose of going through a simple priority-setting exercise is to increase the probability of you being happy with what you select. Extablishing priorities is a widely used practice by business and government. The more one knows about what is important to oneself, the happier that individual will normally be with his/her selection decision.

The software selection priority setting process requires you to first divide the selection criteria into one of the following three categories:

    o   Required - Unless the software possesses this criterion, it will not be considered for selection.

- Desirable - A nonessential criterion, but one that would add to the desirability of the the software and should be considered in the selection process.

- Not applicable (N/A) - The criterion is not wanted, and if included in the software package should not be considered in the selection process.

After all of the selection criteria have been so categorized, then the desirable criteria should be further categorized as follows:

- Highly important - The criterion is not essential but is a very desirable feature of the software.

- Medium importance - The criterion is of interest and would be used but is more of a nicety than what would be ordered if the software package was custom made.

- Low importance - The feature is of some value, but probably would not be used immediately. Criteria falling into this category are features that must either be put into practice to determine if they are worthwhile, or features that have no immediate value but may be valuable in the future.

This book has discussed thirty different selection criteria divided into five categories. In establishing the priorities for these five categories and thirty criteria, the following two options are offered:

Option 1 - Quick Method

The selector can rate each of the five categories in accordance with the previously described priority method. The categories would be evaluated one by one and a decision made as to the priority assigned to that specific category. For example, the restrictions category describes the hardware and software restrictions placed on the selection process. For example, you may already own a 32K computer with two disk drives and use the CP/M operating system. If it is your intention that any software package acquired must run on that configuration, then you would rate the restrictions category as a "required" priority. This would mean that any software package that does not run on that configuration will not be considered. In other words, to get the needed software package you wouldn't consider adding another 32K of storage.

The support, operations, requirements, and cost categories would also be prioritized. For example, you may have established an upper limit for cost, and thus that would be ranked in the "required" priority category; vendor support for you may be a low priority; operations, a medium priority; and requirements, a high priority in the event there are no specific required requirements but what the package can do is more important than the operational ease in which it can be performed.

Option 2 - Systematic Priority Method

Using this option, each of the thirty selection criteria would be individually rated. Each criterion should be individually analyzed, and a determination made of the importance or priority of that selection criteria. At the completion of the exercise, the selected priorities should be documented.

COMPLETING THE SOFTWARE SELECTION WORKSHEET

The worksheet to document the software selection is illustrated in Figure 14. This is a multipurpose worksheet used to both document the priority of the selection criteria, and then to rank competing software packages and their ability to satisfy the selection criteria (Note: The rating of software will be discussed in a later chapter.).

The worksheet is completed as follows:

- o Selection criteria - A listing of the five selection categories and the thirty selection criteria. The individual criteria have been previously explained.

- o Minimum capability - The criteria are general and may need to be further defined before they can be prioritized or rated. For example, the main memory size restriction must be quantified; the ease of use operations criterion needs to be clarified; and the type of fields requirement criterion needs to be defined. The minimum capability column should be used for that clarification or definition.

- o Selection priority - The priority assigned to either the selection category or the individual selection criterion.

SOFTWARE RATED:
1. _____
2. _____
3. _____
4. _____

Figure 14/Software Selection Worksheet

SELECTION CRITERIA	MINIMUM CAPABILITY	SELECTION PRIORITY					RATING				COMMENTS
		REQUIRED	HIGH	MEDIUM	LOW	N/A	1	2	3	4	
RESTRICTIONS 1. Hardware architecture 2. Main memory size 3. Input/output device 4. Operating system SUPPORT 1. Vendor reputation 2. Software training 3. Software service 4. Software enhancements OPERATIONS 1. Menu driven 2. Usable documentation 3. Help routines 4. Adequate data validation 5. Understandable error messages 6. Automatic file backup 7. Report generator 8. Integrated processing 9. Adequate audit trail 10. Forgiving system REQUIREMENTS 1. Needed field types 2. Adequate field size 3. Needed processing capabilities 4. Sufficient storage 5. Ease of retrieval 6. Ease of use 7. Sufficient speed 8. Proper sequence(s) 9. Needed reports 10. Adequate Controls COST 1. Purchase 2. Operate											
SCORE											

o   Rating, comments, and software rated columns - These columns are used in the evaluation process and will be explained in Chapters 7 and 8.

Using the Software Selection Worksheet

This worksheet is meant to simplify the selection process and not complicate it. Both a simple and extended option are available for using the worksheet. The purpose of either option is to help make a logical business decision about an area in which the individual making the decision may only have minimal knowledge.

The selection method presented for software is similar to what major corporations use in determining a site for a new plant or sales office. They first decide what is important in locating the plant, such as sufficient electricity, water, employees with proper skills, etc. These criteria are then prioritized, which is the process we have just finished in our software selection process. Next we must find available software, rate it, and make a software solution decision. This worksheet will be used in these latter selection steps.

> **SOFTWARE SELECTION SURVIVAL RULE #14**
> The amount of effort spent on evaluating software should be directly related to the importance of that software to you.

6
STEP 3—IDENTIFY SOFTWARE ALTERNATIVES

If you don't know what your selection alternatives are you can't make a choice.

Thousands of programs are available for the microcomputers. The number grows larger day by day. This poses the following two related problems in acquiring an application software package:

1) Identifying all the available candidates for the specific set of processing requirements

2) Minimizing the amount of time spent in the software identification process

These software selection problems pose two challenges to the selector. First, if all of the candidate packages are not identified an unnecessary compromise may be made in the selection process. Second, if the software identification process is too time-consuming, the selector may opt not to complete the process and just select a package and run with it.

This chapter is designed to help the individual with selection responsibility through the process of identifying candidate software packages to fulfill the requirements outlined in Step 1 and prioritized in Step 2. The process identifies where software is available, and how to quickly determine whether each of the potential sources can help identify software candidates. Obviously, this assumes that sufficient time has been allocated for the software selection process.

OWNERSHIP OF SOFTWARE

Application software that is sold is developed by an individual or company. As with other products, it is tested, packaged, priced, and marketed. The group developing the software owns it.

Until a few years ago, software could not be copyrighted. While it was recognized that the developer owned the software and had vested rights to the software, the method and process of enforcing those rights was unclear. Today, software can be copyrighted.

The question of copyrighted ownership is important for the following two reasons:

1) Copyright information cannot be copied and passed from person to person without violating the copyright laws.

2) If the software vendor goes out of business, and many do, the software is still protected under the copyright laws. Thus, additional copies of manuals, programs, forms, etc. may not be available from the developer of the software, and yet you are prohibited from copying that information if necessary in order to utilize the software.

Software programs are merely data on a computer file. Most software programs exist on a diskette. In fact, many of the programs will be delivered to you on a diskette. This means that while they cannot legally be copied, the actual copy process is a very simple one. In fact, any computer with two diskette disk drives can easily copy computer software programs.

How Do Companies Protect Software From Being Copied?

All of the industries that sell their product on electronic media, such as record companies, video tape and disk companies, as well as software vendors, recognize the risk of having their product copied. Associated with this risk is a potentially large loss of revenue. For example, suppose you were a member of a computer club of fifty people. If one person in the club bought software they could easily make forty-nine copies and give it to everyone else in the club. Although this is illegal, it can and does happen.

To combat this illegal copying of their software, the software vendors often build self-destruct mechanisms into the software itself. In other words, if you attempt to illegally copy the software the software will self-destruct. Self-destruct means that the electronic media is erased and thus the program is gone.

Some of the methods used to self-destruct programs are:

- o Identify home computer - When the program is first executed, it stores sufficient information to identify the computer on which it is run. Each additional execution then determines if it is being run on the same computer. If the software package cannot recognize the computer on which it is being run, a Trojan Horse routine buried in the program activates and erases the program from disk storage.

o Date monitoring - Programs that are rented instead of purchased can monitor dates stored in the operating system. When the rental contract is renewed the software company or their agent physically modifies the program to search for a new date. If the rental agreement has not been renewed the program erases itself at the end of the rental period.

o Identify copy process - Through some very sophisticated programming, software systems are able to determine when they are being copied. When this is detected the program self-destructs.

Unfortunately for the software developers, as fast as the developers devise ways to prevent the software from being copied other unscrupulous vendors develop ways to circumvent the copy controls. For example, programs with such ingenious names as LOCKSMITH have devised a method of randomly snatching a few bytes from a program at a time so that it can be copied without knowing it's being copied. The reader is cautioned that copying programs is a violation of the copyright law and subjects the copier to legal sanctions.

So How Do I Safeguard My Software?

One of the golden rules of computer processing is to make backup copies of data and programs. Backup copies are backed up, and backup backup copies are backed up. In data processing this is known as the grandfather, father, and son approach. If the son is lost, the father can step in with the needed data and programs, and if both the son and father are lost, the grandfather steps into the gap.

This concept presupposes that both programs and data can be copied. If programs cannot be copied they cannnot be backed up, and if the single source of the program is lost the program is lost. As previously discussed, a program could be destroyed because:

1) Hardware failure
2) Diskette, disk, or disk drive failure
3) Operator error
4) Application programmer operating system error

When a software program is selected, the following questions need to be asked to determine first if the program can be copied for backup purposes, and if not what is the customer to do if the program is inadvertently destroyed:

1) Is the software program copyright? (If not, it can be copied.)

2) Does the application package being acquired have self-destruct routines in the software? (If so, it is necessary to determine how another copy of the program can be acquired, should the original version be destroyed--and how quickly that copy can be obtained.)

3) Can the program be copied for one's personal use? (Again, if not, how does the customer protect himself against inadvertent software destruction?)

> **SOFTWARE SELECTION SURVIVAL RULE #15**
> Get what you can free, buy what you can't get as a gift--and make backup copies of everything.

IDENTIFYING SOFTWARE CANDIDATES

Software for the microcomputer is growing in both numbers and capabilities. With the large number of software packages and the divergence of needs, it is an impossible task for any one individual or organization, such as a computer store, to keep abreast of this rapidly changing field. However, the computer without software is of no value, making it a necessary task for the computer user to search out the needed software.

Locating software should be approached in a systematic manner to minimize effort and maximize the identification of candidates to satisfy the user needs. The following process is recommended to simplify this process:

o   Task 1 - Keep abreast of software trends and announcements - Once you own a computer you are in a rapidly changing field. Time spent studying the field and monitoring current events establishes a framework for conducting the selection process based on knowledge of the type of software available in microcomputer uses.

o   Task 2 - Identify sources of software - Identify where software can be acquired and become familiar with those sources of software and the types of software they stock.

o   Task 3 - Categorize your requirements as a basis for identifying software candidates - Determine what type or category of software you are attempting to locate.

o   Task 4 - Identify software location - Through telephone calls, mail, and personal inquiries develop a list of software packages that appear to meet your specific needs. This list will be used in conducting the evaluation to identify the software solution.

Task 1 - Keep Abreast of Software Trends and Announcements

The computer is one of the most versatile tools available for processing information. The more you learn about the computer, the more uses you will find for this tool. Computer users find that as their learning increases so does the number of potential uses for using the computer in their profession or job.

The cheapest method to keep abreast of the computer field is to subscribe to one or more computer publications. This continual stream of computer knowledge will keep you informed of how people are using computers, new technical capabilities, as well as the types of software available and where to acquire that software.

A list and brief explanation of the purpose of many of the more popular microcomputer periodicals is listed in Figure 15. You will note that some are directed toward specific hardware, some toward a particular class of users, while others are more general in nature. Many of these magazines are available for inspection in computer stores, and some in public libraries. If not easily available for inspection, you may want to write to the publisher for a sample copy or to purchase a single copy to find if it contains the type of information that would be helpful to you in keeping up to date on what is happening in Computerland.

Other methods for acquiring basic computer skills, and keeping up to date on the state of the art in computer technology are:

- o   Computer courses at community colleges (note that many of these provide for hands-on experience)

- o   Visit one or more computer stores to see, touch, and experience using a computer

- o   Attend a computer fair

Figure 15/Microcomputer Periodicals

Access, "The Journal of Microcomputer Applications" - Box 12847, Research Triangle Park, NC 27709
    Journal covering use and applications of microcomputers.

Byte Magazine - 70 Main St., Peterborough, NH 03458
    General personal computer magazine published monthly for college-educated computer users.

Compute! - Small System Services, Box 5406, 652 Fulton St., Greensboro, NC 27403
    Monthly magazine covering the application of personal computers in homes, schools, and other cunsumer settings.

Creative Computing - 39 E. Hanover Ave., Morris Plains, NJ 07950
    Monthly magazine covering the use and effects of computers in homes, businesses, and schools.

Desktop Computing - 80 Pine St., Peterborough, NH 03458
    Monthly publication covering computer applications for homes and small businesses.

80 Microcomputing - 80 Magazine St., Peterborough, NH 03458
    Monthly magazine about microcomputing for owners and users of Radio Shack's TRS-80.

Figure 15/Microcomputer Periodicals (cont'd)

Infoworld, "The Newsweekly for Microcomputer Users" - Popular Computing, Inc., 530 Lytton Ave., Suite 303, Palo Alto, CA 94301

>Tabloid covering small-computer use in homes, businesses, and classrooms.

Interactive Computing, "The Journal of the Association of Computer Users" - ACU Research & Education Division, Box 9003, Boulder, CO 80301

>General monthly magazine covering computers and offering user-oriented advice.

Interface Age, "Computing for Business and Home" - McPheters, Wolfe & Jones, 16704 Marquardt Ave., Cerritos, CA 90701

>Monthly magazine covering home computers.

Micro Discovery, "The Non-Technical Magazine of Personal Computing" - Micro Digest, Inc., Box 9118, Fountain Valley, CA 92708

>Monthly magazine covering home computers.

Micro, "The 6502/6809 Journal" - MICRO INK, Inc., 34 Chelmsford St., Chelmsford, MA 01824

>Monthly magazine covering applications, programming techniques, aids, and resources for the intermediate to advanced 6502 or 6809 microcomputer user.

Figure 15/Microcomputer Periodicals (cont'd)

Microcomputer Index - 2464 El Camino Real, Suite 247, Santa Clara, CA 95051
> Index with abstracts and summaries published quarterly and covering more than thirty magazines.

Microcomputing - 73 Magazine St., Peterborough, NH 03458
> Monthly magazine.

PC: The Independent Guide to IBM Personal Computers - Software Communications, 1528 Irving St., San Francisco, CA 94122
> Monthly publication that includes product reviews, applications information, and user reports for IBM computerists.

Personal Computer Age, "The Definitive Journal for the IBM Personal Computer User" - Box 70725, Pasadena, CA 91107
> Monthly journal featuring news and applications for owners of IBM personal computers.

Personal Computing - Hayden Publishing Co., 50 Essex St., Rochelle Park, NJ 07662
> Monthly magazine covering home, small businesses, and school computing.

Popular Computing Magazine - 70 Main St., Peterborough, NH 03458
> Monthly magazine covering personal computers directed specifically toward beginners, and professionals such as lawyers, educators, doctors, etc.

Figure 15/Microcomputer Periodicals (cont'd)

Programmers Software exchange - 2110 N. 2nd St., Cabot, AZ 72023
  Quarterly magazine covering peronal computers.

Syntax ZX80 - Syntax ZX80, Inc., Rt. 2, Box 457, Bolton Rd., Harvard, MA 01451
  Monthly newsletter covering ZX80, ZX81, and MicroAce microcomputers.

Word Processing News: A Writer's POV on Word Processing - 1765 N. Highland Ave., #306-IW, Hollywood, CA 90028
  Bimonthly newsletter for computerists who work with words.

Excerpt from "Writing Made Easier with Personal Computers," *Writers Digest,* September 1982, pp 33-42. Reprinted with permission of *Writers Digest.*

o   Acquire and read books on data processing (note that many hardware vendors and publishers provide introductory books on data processing)

o   Attend professional seminars (Note: As soon as you purchase a computer or subscribe to a computer periodical, you will start receiving notices about professional computer seminars.)

Task 2 - Identify Sources of Software

The most common source of software for the novice is the computer store. In fact, many beginners in the computer field think that the computer store is the only source of application software. This is not the case. There are many good sources to acquire software.

If one was looking for an automobile you wouldn't only go to a new car showroom to acquire an automobile. You know that you can also acquire automobiles from a used-car lot, automobile rental agencies, friends, through the classified section of the newspaper, and through automobile auctions. The sources of software are just as varied as the sources of automobiles.

The most common sources for computer software are:

o   The computer store - A retail establishment that sells, leases, and maintains computer hardware and software.

Some of these computer stores are located in shopping centers, while others are located in offices, such as marketing representatives of hardware and software vendors who sell by telephone, visit your place of business or you can visit their place of business.

o   Advertisements/mail order - As the number of microcomputers increases, more software is being advertised and marketed through the mail or via telephone. If you purchase a computer, software package, or one of the many computer publications you may be bombarded with software promotional material through your home mailbox.

Sources of advertisements for computer software can be found in:

- Computer magazines/newsletters
- General business publications
- Business section of local newspapers
- Brochures (located in computer stores or mailed to you)
- Attached to computer hardware and other software packages

o   User groups/clubs - Groups of people having common hardware or computer interest band together into user groups or clubs. The more common computer user groups are associated with a specific hardware vendor like Apple

Computing. Some of these clubs maintain libraries of software, some of which may be donated by the vendor and other members in the club. Frequently, the software is available at nominal cost, such as the purchase price and mailing cost of a diskette. Some clubs market software of interest to their users, while other clubs provide a vehicle for members to market software to other club members.

It is generally a good investment to join a computer club if one is provided for your make of computer. Because of the potentially large software library available from these user groups and other information provided by them, the existence of a users group might be a major factor in deciding which computer hardware to acquire.

o   Friends - You probably already have, or will acquire, friends who have the same computer or software needs as you have. These friends can provide you with copies of noncopyrighted software as well as sources for acquiring software. If you don't know anyone with the same computer or software interests that you have, contact the individual from whom you bought your hardware or software for a list of names. Most computer users want to maintain some contact with other users, and are normally receptive to periodic phone calls and/or get-togethers to discuss common problems and needs.

- Consultants - The computer field is alive with consultants. Many of these consultants have developed and market software. Normally their software is special purpose, such as job- and industry-oriented software. For example, many CPA firms have software available for sale to help with financial accounting and financial modeling.

    Consulting firms are now being organized to help the small computer user. These consultants hold classes, help users find and select software, as well as write or provide software for them. Generally there is no cost to make an inquiry to consultants about their services and available software.

- Computer fairs - A must for computer users is attendance at a computer fair. Some of these fairs are national, sponsored by users groups, while others are local events, sponsored and produced by computer stores and other vendors of hardware and software. These fairs are designed specifically for the microcomputer as a means of explaining and demonstrating microcomputer hardware and software.

    The fair provides an opportunity for those having products and wanting to sell them to meet those having computer hardware and software needs. Normally there is a nominal charge to attend the computer fair, but most computer stores offer discount coupons which either provide free admission or reduce the cost of attendance. Computer fairs are a very effective way to find out what software is available for your computer. They also provide an opportunity to meet other users and to learn about publications, user groups, and computer consultants.

Computer fairs are normally promoted:

- By computer stores
- In the business section of local newspapers
- In a "fair" section, listed in computer publications
- Through direct mail from computer consultants and vendors

o   Hardware vendor - The same manufacturer that makes the computer hardware may also make computer software. At a minimum, the hardware vendors either provide or make provisions for owners to acquire operating systems. Some hardware manufacturers offer hundreds of software programs, so that it should not be overlooked as a source of software. Some vendors provide newsletters which indicate software available and where it can be acquired, as well as advise their customers of the more common places to acquire software for their computer.

o   Self-developed (software) - A previously stated computer rule was "If all else fails, read the directions." This can be restated in the software selection process as "When all else fails, write your own programs." This obviously requires programming skills, but with some of the simpler languages and some limited training most people can write computer programs.

Programming languages can be categorized into those designed specifically for the small computer and those designed for the larger computer to solve more complex problems. Although it is more difficult today to state that a small computer can't solve a big problem, what we are really talking about is programming languages for those with minimal skills and programming languages for those who make their living writing programs.

The two computer languages that are most common on the microcomputers and that require the least skills are:

-   BASIC (Beginners All-Purpose Symbolic Instruction Code) - One of the easiest programming languages to understand, learn, and use. It is probably the most widely used languange for the small computer. Unfortunately, there are many versions of BASIC and not all programs are interchangeable.

-   Pascal (named for famous French physicist and philosopher, Blaise Pascal) - Pascal is a highly structured, high-level programming languange that is becoming a standard of the industry due to its self-documenting features. It is useful in teaching computer programming as it helps find programming errors quickly. The language has no defaults and can be used on most computers.

The three computer languages that have widely accepted usage among the professional programming group are:

- COBOL (COmmon Business-Oriented Language) - This is a commercial programming language used to handle large amounts of data. COBOL-produced programs normally are more efficient than programs written in BASIC or Pascal.

- FORTRAN (FORmula TRANslater) - Primarily a scientific language for use in defining and solving mathematical problems. Generally not a good language for writing business programs.

- PL/1 (Programming Language 1) - A language designed to incorporate the characteristics of both COBOL and FORTRAN into one language.

Program-Writing Process

Writing your own software is generally the last resort for the microcomputer user. On the other hand, programming can be fun, and a lot of people enjoy programming for the sake of programming. If the individuals become good at programming, and if they do not put a price tag on their own time, they can save money by writing the software themselves. However, if you were to put a price tag on your own time it would be almost impossible to write an application program for less than the purchase price of an equivalent package.

The steps that you would have to follow in writing a program are:

o   Step 1 - Define output requirements

   The programming process commences with the definition of the results required from a program. This is usually expressed in reports or other outputs. Programmers "mock up" what the reports produced by the program will look like, and these become the detailed program requirements.

o   Step 2 - Define input and processing

   The data required to produce the reports must be defined, as well as the processing that must occur to create the output reports from the input data.

o   Step 3 - Flowchart program logic

   A desirable, but not essential, step is to draw a flowchart of the programming logic, which shows how the input data is transformed to output reports. A flowchart is a pictorial representation of the program specifications developed in Step 1 and 2 above.

o   Step 4 - Code the program

Using the program flowchart as the program specification, the programming process must translate the program specifications into program code. This is the equivalent of translating from one language to another, for example, from French to English. Programming languages are just that-- another language used to express computer programs.

o   Step 5 - Compile program

Each language comes with its own compiler, which can translate a language understood by people into a language understood by machines. All of the above five programming languages were designed for people to use. Unfortunately, computers can't understand that language so whichever language is used to code the program must be translated or compiled into a language that the computer can understand. The computer language is normally referred to as machine language. (Isn't that a neat name for a language a machine can understand?)

o   Step 6 - Test program

Surprise, surprise--computer programs don't always work. If

you don't know that now, you will soon. This is because even the simplest of programs have literally hundreds of thousands of different paths through the program. The program testing step is designed to verify that at least the most commonly used paths through the program work. To perform this step, the developer of the program uses the program in a test mode. Test transactions are entered, and the results are evaluated to determine whether or not they are correct. If the results from testing are correct, the program is ready for use; however, if the results are incorrect, then some or all of the above steps must be repeated depending on where the problem occurred.

Task 3 - Categorize Your Requirements

A previous section identified the four most popular types or categories of software. For the purpose of identifying where software is located, the following eight categories will be used:

1) Operating system - The software package that directs operation within the computer. Some computers use a common operating system, such as CP/M, while other computers have specialized operating systems developed by the hardware manufacturer.

2) Data management and utilities - The acquisition, storage, organization, and retrieval of data is one of the most time-consuming functions performed by the computer. It is also a

repetitious function in that the same tasks are performed repetitively. Because large amounts of resources are spent executing common tasks, software has been developed that generalizes many of those functions. These generalized software packages fall into the two general categories of data management systems and utility programs.

The data management systems are frequently called data base management systems. This software permits data to be managed independently of the applications that use that data. Using this concept, many programs can utilize this common set of data, and in advanced systems two or more programs can use the same data concurrently. It is through the use of data base management systems (frequently called DBMS) that the full power of integrated processing can be achieved.

Utility programs are generalized routines to perform common functions. These routines can prepare reports from most types of computer files, resequence and perform maintenance on data files, as well as perform limited generalized processing capabilities. Most computer installations find the need for utility programs after a short time in operation. These are very effective ways to perform routine tasks, particularly those that may only be performed once, or infrequently. Most operating systems come with several utility programs.

3) Accounting - Systems that prepare information for and produce financial statements.

4) Games - Software for fun and enjoyment.

5) Word processing - Software systems used in the development of letters, reports, and manuscripts. The more common features of word processing programs are formatting, error correction, structuring of information, merging information from multiple sources, as well as spelling and syntax checking.

6) Educational - Software designed to teach you basic and technical skills. Most skills that can be taught in the classroom can be taught through computer-aided instruction, although the techniques used in many computerized educational courses are still very basic.

7) Personal - Software designed to perform or aid in the performance of personal tasks, such as check writing, budgeting, and recipe modification for different-sized batches.

8) Specialized for job/industry - Programs oriented toward specific jobs or industries, such as medical practice accounting, motel registration, and job cost accounting.

In the selection of software, it is good practice to categorize the needed software into one of the above categories, as a basis for further identification. For example, if you are looking for a system to help you prepare documents the starting point is to categorize that requirement as a word processing type of program. If you are looking for software that will simulate and attack space invaders, you start by categorizing the request as a game.

Task 4 - Identify Software Location

Some sources of software are best known for specific types of software. For example, the hardware vendor is one of the few suppliers of operating systems, while consultants may specialize in job- or industry-oriented programs.

As an aid in locating desired software, a Software Location Matrix (see Figure 16) is presented. This matrix shows the most common locations or sources of software, plus the common categories of software. The intersection of the matrix shows which locations are the best sources for which categories of software. For example, you might use self-developed programs for personal and specialized job/industry software, and if you were searching for word processing software, your best sources to find it would be computer stores, advertisements, computer fairs, and hardware vendors. The matrix is presented as a tool to assist in the software location task.

Figure 16/Software Location Matrix

LOCATION OF SOFTWARE \ CATEGORIES OF SOFTWARE	OPERATING SYSTEM	DATA MANAGEMENT AND UTILITIES	ACCOUNTING	GAMES	WORD PROCESSING	EDUCATIONAL	PERSONAL	SPECIALIZED FOR JOB/INDUSTRY
Computer Stores		✓	✓	✓	✓	✓	✓	✓
Advertisements		✓	✓	✓	✓	✓	✓	✓
User groups/Clubs				✓				✓
Friends				✓			✓	✓
Consultants		✓	✓					✓
Computer fairs		✓	✓	✓	✓	✓	✓	✓
Hardware vendor	✓	✓	✓	✓	✓	✓	✓	
Self-developed							✓	✓

> **SOFTWARE SELECTION SURVIVAL RULE #16**
> You must first have a need and then second locate the best software to satisfy that need before purchasing any software.

7
STEP 4—COMPARE SOFTWARE PACKAGES

If you can find a better software package—buy it!

The object of this step is to compare the software packages identified as potential candidates to satisfy your requirements, against those requirements. If only a single software package is available, the question is one of whether or not that package will sufficiently satisfy your requirements. If two or more software packages are potential candidates, then not only must it be determined whether or not each of those candidate software packages can satisfy your needs, but which among them does it the best.

This chapter explains the methods you can use to compare the characteristics of software packages against your requirements. Included in the chapter are the necessary questions, checklists, and the tasks that you should perform. The results of that comparison should be recorded on the Software Selection Worksheet (Figure 14).

METHODS FOR EVALUATING SOFTWARE CHARACTERISTICS

The recommended evaluation process uses the evaluation criteria you established in Step 2 of the software selection process. At the completion of Step 2 you had identified both the criteria and the priority in which you wanted to evaluate that criteria. You can perform that evaluation in any one or a combination of the following four evaluation methods:

o   Method 1 - Inquiry - You talk with the group offering the software to determine its characteristics and how it compares against your evaluation criteria.

o   Method 2 - Study manuals/promotional material - Acquire the software specifications and instructions and through analysis of those specifications assess the ability of the software capabilities to satisfy your processing requirements.

o   Method 3 - Obtain testimonials/evaluations - Call or visit users of the software to determine how it functions in their environment, or obtain documented evaluations of the software package from reputable sources. Compare this information against your evaluation criteria.

o   Method 4 - Conduct software demonstration - Through demonstration or personal usage, determine whether the software meets your evaluation criteria.

Each of these four methods is individually explained. A method is proposed to assist you in determining how closely your evaluation criterion is met. This evaluation will enable you to rate each criterion so that in the final evaluation step you can develop a simple numeric score for use in selecting your software solution.

> **SOFTWARE SELECTION SURVIVAL RULE #17**
> What you see is what you get; so if you don't evaluate the software you deserve what you get.

METHOD 1 - INQUIRY

Inquiry is the easiest, fastest, but normally the least effective method for performing software evaluation. However, the inquiry method can be strengthened if you have completed the Show and Tell Requirements Worksheet (Figure 12) and the Software Evaluation Selection Worksheet (Figure 14) and use them as a basis for an oral investigation.

The inquiry or oral investigation is an interview with a knowledgeable person about the software in question. This can occur in a computer store, a visit with a software vendor representative, or a telephone interview. The objective of the inquiry is to gather sufficient information to perform the evaluation.

The oral inquiry has the following disadvantages:

- Both questions and answers may be misunderstood
- Oral claims may be later denied on the grounds of misunderstanding
- Obvious disadvantages may be overlooked because either you or the vendor representative neglected to address those areas

The oral inquiry should be conducted as follows:

o   Task 1 - Complete list of requirements and evaluation criteria.

o   Task 2 - Address the evaluation criteria item by item, starting with the required criteria and continuing from high to low priority. If at any point it becomes obvious the software will not meet requirements, terminate the interview on the software package.

o   Task 3 - Document the results of the interview.

METHOD 2 - STUDY MANUALS/PROMOTIONAL MATERIAL

Almost all software comes with a user manual which may be summarized in promotional brochures. In addition, manuals on how to service it may be prepared for the people marketing the software. As much of this material as is available should be gathered and studied.

The objective in analyzing the manuals is to identify the operating characteristics of the software in order to evaluate the characteristics of the software against your requirements. The instruction manuals are normally written by the developers of the software, or in conjunction with the developers of the software. Normally there is more information available in the software users manual than will be known by marketing personnel. In fact, a good marketing person would most likely refer to the users manual during the oral interview.

Reviewing the users manual is a good way to learn how to operate the software and what it can accomplish, but has the following disadvantages:

- o   Detailed users manual may not be available

- o   It takes some EDP skills and a reasonable amount of time to study the manuals in enough detail to obtain the needed evaluation information

- o   Manuals may be inaccurate

- o   Manuals may be out of date (in both this and the preceding disadvantage the documentation may state that the software performs a function when, in fact, it does not)

The suggested method for evaluating documentation in order to evaluate software is:

- o   Task 1 - Obtain from the software vendor, or marketer of the software, as much documentation as you can get on the software.

- o   Task 2 - Define the software selection criteria (Figure 14) and review the documentation only to obtain the information necessary to determine whether or not the software achieves those criteria (don't waste your time reading and learning about software).

o Task 3 - Document the results of the interview.

METHOD 3 - OBTAIN TESTIMONIALS/EVALUATIONS

Application software is evaluated by the following groups:

o   Publishers of computer periodicals and journals

o   Consultants

o   Vendors to show the strengths and weaknesses of their software against their competitors

o   Users of the software

o   User groups

Some of these evaluations are performed by highly skilled people in an unbiased manner and present an excellent overview of the capabilities, advantages, and disadvantages of acquiring a piece of software. These reviews are similar to having a movie or book reviewed by a critic. If you have faith in the critic, following that person's advice may save you both the expense of purchasing a ticket to a movie or play, or buying a book, or the time invested in watching television. The same is true of the software which will be of little or no value to you.

The advantage of obtaining an assessment from an independent third party is both the insight of a skilled individual and the time you save by not having to perform the evaluation personally. While it is always advisable to obtain an independent third-party review, even if you don't rely on it, these reviews have the following disadvantages:

- o   The reviewer may be prejudiced for or against software by this vendor

- o   The reviewer may not take into account the skill level of the user

- o   The reviewer may not address some of the specific concerns or criteria that are important to your evaluation criteria

Using a third-party assessment poses two dilemmas. The first is where to obtain the reviews, and second, how to assess the skill and impartiality of the reviewer. The following method is recommended to address those concerns in using third-party evaluations:

- o   Task 1 - Obtain from the group marketing the software any evaluations they have (they are normally glad to give you good evaluations, but will not give you bad evaluations), and a list of three or four references of people who have acquired and are using the software.

- Task 2 - Find a competitor for the software in consideration, and ask the competitor for evaluations.

- Task 3 - Contact the references provided and ask them for a personal assessment as well as their knowledge of any independent assessments of the software.

- Task 4 - Contact computer professional groups, such as a users group for your computer hardware, and ask them who performs assessments of software and contact those parties for that assessment. (Note that independent groups such as Datapro perform professional hardware and software assessments, but these services are very expensive and normally out of the reach of the small computer user).

- Task 5 - Use the independent evaluations to answer as many evaluation criteria as possible. If the major evaluation criteria are not addressed in the review, call individuals who use the software to get answers for those specific criteria.

- Task 6 - Document the results of the interview.

METHOD 4 - CONDUCT SOFTWARE DEMONSTRATION

The ultimate test and evaluation method is to use the software. This is by far the strongest evaluation method, particularly if you have clearly established in your mind the requirements that you want the software to meet.

Normally, the demonstration will occur in a computer store or a vendor's place of business. Occasionally, you may be offered the software on trial, in which case you can perform the assessment at your leisure in your own place of business.

It is strongly recommended that you evaluate software through the demonstration process. Much more can be learned from watching and testing application software on the computer than from the other methods. However, a demonstration does have the following potential disadvantages:

- o If performed by vendor personnel, some relatively difficult tasks may look simple, and the vendor person may avoid demonstrating functions that are poorly performed by the software.

- o If the demonstration is performed in the vendor's place of business, you may be under pressure to conclude the demonstration.

- o The hardware on which the software is demonstrated may have features that are or will not be available on your computer, which makes the software easier or faster to operate.

o A thorough and proper demonstration will require both preparatory time and, perhaps, several hours on the computer.

If you are serious about a particular software package the time expended in performing the demonstration will be very worthwhile. If you select the package, the demonstration will have given you some preliminary training on the package, and even if you choose not to select it it will solidify your list of software requirements.

The recommended method for evaluating computer software through a demonstration is:

o Task 1 - Define requirements. Prior to conducting the demonstration it is important to know the specific objectives of the demonstraion. In other words, what type of assessments must you perform in order to ensure whether or not the software meets your objectives?

o Task 2 - Make a demonstration appointment. A well-performed demonstration will take from one to four hours to complete. If you are going to do the test, and do it right, lay out what you hope to accomplish and then ask for sufficient time to properly perform the evaluation.

o Task 3 - Obtain instruction manual ahead of demonstration. Not only should the computer time be reserved, but you should take sufficient time to learn how to use the computer software prior to the demonstration. If you cannot obtain the manual for any time span, visit the computer demonstration area an hour or two prior to the demonstration so you can become familiar with the documentation.

o   Task 4 - Outline in detail the tasks that you want to perform. By knowing exactly what you want to do prior to the demonstration, not only do you find the answers to your evaluation criteria, but you reduce the amount of time required to perform the evaluation exercise and through preparedness make the computer vendor more willing to allot you the necessary time.

o   Task 5 - Conduct the demonstration. During the demonstration you should be observant for both the operating characteristics of the software, and its accomplishment or lack of accomplishment of your evaluation objectives. Checklist 2 is a questionnaire for you to use during the demonstration process. The questions included on this figure are general questions, which should be supplemented by questions regarding the tests you want to perform. Yes answers are indicative of good software and no answers, poor software. Add comments on the questionnaire where appropriate.

o   Task 6 - Document the results.

CHECKLIST 2

DEMONSTRATION EVALUATION CHECKLIST

#	ITEM	YES	NO	N/A	COMMENTS
1.	Is the program easy to load into the computer?	✓			Floppy disk - put in drive - turn on - brings up menu on screen - Menu
2.	Does the program adequately identify itself?	✓			
3.	Are the menus easy to follow?	✓			
4.	Do the menus identify all the major software capabilities?	✓			
5.	Are the screens easy to read?	✓			
6.	Is the wording on the screens clear?	✓			
7.	If you make a mistake of what step to take, is help easy to get in the form of a help screen or instructions in a workbook?	✓			

CHECKLIST 2

(continued)

ITEM	RESPONSE			
	YES	NO	N/A	COMMENTS
8. Is it easy to enter input data?	✓			
9. Are the input fields big enough for the information you will need to enter into these fields?	✓			
10. Are there adequate diagnostics to ensure that you entered the data correctly?		✓		
11. If you make an error entering data, is it clear as to what type made, and on what field the error was made?	✓			yes because of automatic balancing of accounts it will flag you
12. Is the processing performed in the sequence in which you want to perform the tasks?				
13. Does the amount of time required to process the transactions seem reasonable?				
14. Are the keyboard procedures easy to execute?				

CHECKLIST 2

(continued)

ITEM	YES	NO	N/A	COMMENTS
15. Are the output reports easy to interpret?	✓			
16. Do the output reports (or screens) contain the type of information needed for your job?				
17. Are the fields large enough to include the the information you need?				
18. Are the reports or screens in the proper sequence?				
19. Are there adequate controls to ensure that all data entered is processed?				Yes. on reports but must start from beginning — but reprint report.
20. Can processing be stopped in the middle and restarted?				
21. Is processing in main memory backed up at frequent intervals?				No automatic backup — do it yourself blank floppy disk — make a copy

CHECKLIST 2
(continued)

ITEM	RESPONSE			
	YES	NO	N/A	COMMENTS
22. Is the user manual easy to read?				
23. Does the software accomplish all of your processing requirements?				

DOCUMENTING THE RESULTS OF THE SOFTWARE EVALUATION PROCESS

During the evaluation process, a scorecard should be maintained on the software being evaluated. This scorecard indicates how well the software performed in each of the evaluation criteria.

The Software Selection Worksheet (Figure 14) should be used as the evaluation scorecard. The worksheet provides space to record the assessment made for each of the evaluation criteria. The assessment process requires you to rate each of the assessment criteria.

Rating the Software Package

During the evaluation process, each of the evaluation criteria should be assessed. This book has identified thirty potential selection criteria. However, all of these may not be important and thus the actual selection criteria may be a lesser number.

In evaluating each of the thirty selection criteria, you should put the priority that you assign to each criterion in the selection priority column of Figure 14. This can be done with a check mark and should be completed during Step 2. The N/A column represents criteria which will not be considered in the selection process.

The ratings assigned will vary depending upon whether the criterion is a required or desirable criterion. Required criteria must be included in the software for it to be considered for acquisition, while desirable criteria need not be present.

The required selection rating will be one of the following two:

- o Pass - The software meets the required selection criteria.

- o Fail - The software being evaluated does not meet the minimum processing requirements.

The desired criteria are rated in one of the following four categories:

- o Fully satisfactory - The criteria requirements have been fully met.

- o Satisfactory - The requirements can be achieved, but in a less than fully efficient or effective manner.

- o Less than satisfactory - The requirements can be partially satisfied.

- o Unsatisfactory - The desired feature is either missing or implemented in such a manner that it is not useful.

Guidelines are provided in Figure 17 on how to make these assessments for each of the thirty criteria. While these are general guidelines, they should prove valuable in helping assess the effectiveness and efficiency of a software package.

Figure 17/Suggested Software Selection Criteria Assessments

SELECTION CRITERIA	FULLY SATISFACTORY	SATISFACTORY	LESS THAN SATISFACTORY	UNSATISFACTORY
RESTRICTIONS				
1. Hardware architecture	Runs on existing hardware	Not applicable for this criterion	Requires upgrade of CP	Requires new computer
2. Main memory size	Runs within existing memory	Runs, but requires inefficient use of storage	Requires additional storage to be purchased	Cannot run on existing hardware
3. Input/output devices	Runs using existing input/output devices	Runs, but ineffectively on existing input/output devices	Requires additional input/output devices	Cannot be run using existing computer
4. Operating system	Runs using existing operating system	Runs, but less efficient on existing operating system	Runs on existing hardware, but requires new operating system	Requires the acquisition of new hardware
SUPPORT				
1. Vendor reputation	Outstanding reputation in market place	Good reputation in market place	New vendor or existence of numerous unsatisfied customers	Poor reputation in market place
2. Software training	Fully satisfactory — provides classes, instruction manuals, and automated training with software	Provides instruction manual and automated training with software	Provides instruction manual	No training
3. Software service	Services in your place of business within a reasonable time span	Services in vendor's place of business in a reasonable time span	Telephone or mail service only	No software service
4. Software enhancements	New version to be issued within six months	New version to be issued within twelve months	New version probable, but no time frame	No enhancements planned

-194-

Figure 17/Suggested Software Selection Criteria Assessments (cont'd)

SELECTION CRITERIA	FULLY SATISFACTORY	SATISFACTORY	LESS THAN SATISFACTORY	UNSATISFACTORY
OPERATIONS				
1. Menu driven	All functions described and selected on menus	Major functions selected by menu	Initial menu only	No menus
2. Usable documentation	Documentation provided in step-by-step format with many illustrations	Documentation contains many illustrations	Narrative documentation only	Documentation for marketing purposes only
3. Help routines	Help routines provided for both training and error correction	Help routines provided for training and use of software	Help routines reference training manual	No help routines
4. Adequate data validation	Validates individual data values, reasonable checks and relationship checks	Validates data values and reasonableness of the data values	Validates data values only	No data validation checks
5. Understandable error messages	Provides error messages which are explained in a reference manual, together with most probable causes	Provides error messages which are explained in manuals	Provides error messages	No error messages provided
6. Automatic file backup	Backup provided approximately every five minutes	Backup provided approximately every fifteen minutes	Backup provided by manual request only	No backup included in the software
7. Report generator	Complete report writing option included in software	Format and sequence of existing reports can be changed	Format of existing reports can be changed	User cannot change reports

-195-

Figure 17/Suggested Software Selection Criteria Assessments (cont'd)

SELECTION CRITERIA	FULLY SATISFACTORY	SATISFACTORY	LESS THAN SATISFACTORY	UNSATISFACTORY
8. Integrated processing	Uses data base management concepts	Data automatically passed to related applications	User can indicate transfer of data from application to application	User must manually enter data into related applications
9. Adequate audit trail	Special audit trail file containing before and after images	Special audit trail file	Audit trail data included within transaction processing file	No audit trail
10. Forgiving system	Forgives data deletion, improper processing and errors	Forgives data deletion and improper processing	Forgives data deletion	No forgiveness in software
REQUIREMENTS				
1. Needed field types	All needed field types included	All essential field types included	Some manual processing could compensate for missing field types	Needed processing could not occur
2. Adequate field size	All fields have sufficient space to store information	All key fields are sufficient in size	Processing could occur by dividing values in processing to transactions	Certain types of processing could not occur
3. Needed processing capabilities	Full processing capabilities included	Key processing capabilities included	Processing could be performed using some manual steps	Software fails to meet processing capabilities
4. Sufficient storage	Main storage, permanent and transaction file storage adequate	Transaction and/or permanent file storage can be accomplished using two diskettes	Processing must be split to accomplish on existing storage capacity	Restricted storage prohibits adequate processing

Figure 17/Suggested Software Selection Criteria Assessments (cont'd)

SELECTION CRITERIA	FULLY SATISFACTORY	SATISFACTORY	LESS THAN SATISFACTORY	UNSATISFACTORY
5. Ease of retrieval	Needed information can be retrieved in desired sequence	Needed information can be retrieved but may require additional processing for proper sequence	Some data can be retrieved	No data except that presented in reports can be retrieved
6. Ease of use	No EDP, application, or concentration skills required	No EDP or application skills required	No EDP skills required	EDP, application, and concentration skills required
7. Sufficient Speed	Needed data processed on time economically	Needed data processed on time	Key data processed on time	Information not available when needed
8. Proper sequence(s)	Data files available in multiple sequencing	Data files available in desired sequence	Data files can be put into proper sequence by extra processing	Data not in proper sequence
9. Needed reports	Software produces both needed and optional reports	Software produces needed reports	Needed reports can be obtained with extra processing	Needed reports are missing
10. Adequate controls	Controls ensure that all data entered into the system is processed	Full integrity controls are included but are optional	User can develop controls to prove integrity of processing	No integrity controls included
COST				
1. Purchase	Within cost budget	Slightly over budget but acceptable	Considerably over budget--causes budget to be reevaluated	Cost prohibitive
2. Operate	Within cost budget	Slightly over budget but acceptable	Considerably over budget--causes budget to be reevaluated	Cost prohibitive

-197-

The Software Selection Worksheet is completed by recording the assessment made for each criterion being evaluated. The assessment category selected should be that which most closely fits the software package. After the assessment category is determined it should be recorded on the Software Selection Worksheet (Figure 14) for each software package as follows:

F = fully satisfactory
S = satisfactory
L = less than satisfactory
U = unsatisfactory

OR

P = pass (generally fully satisfactory or satisfactory)
F = fail (generally less than satisfactory or unsatisfactory)

> **SOFTWARE SELECTION SURVIVAL RULE # 18**
> Would you pay $200 to buy a suit or dress you had never seen? Ask your fellow computer users how many software packages they own that they never use. The answer to that question will make you an advocate of a formal software selection process.

8
STEP 5—SELECT THE SOFTWARE SOLUTION

All's well that ends well in the software selection process

The objective of the selection process is to identify the best possible software to meet your processing requirements. If the process has been performed properly all that is needed to do now is to add up the score. Time and effort expended in the earlier steps make this one easy.

This chapter explains the alternatives available for making a software decision. The recommended method is to assign a mathematical value to each evaluation criterion and then accumulate those values to develop an evaluation score. The software package with the highest score is the one selected.

THE DECISION-MAKING PROCESS

Many people find decisions difficult to make, and the decision-making process painful. Experience shows that there is a direct relationship between the amount of effort put into evaluation and the ease of the decision-making process. When the evaluation process is properly performed, the decision is normally obvious.

Decisions are made using one of the four following methods:

METHOD 1 - JUDGEMENT

Judgment is closely allied to a "gut feeling" approach as to which is the correct software package. Judgment is normally based on experience and intuition. This method works best when the individual has had extensive experience in the area in which the decision is to be made. Unfortunately, many people who have to select software have only limited experience, so that the judgment method becomes more of a guess than a decision based on extensive experience.

METHOD 2 - DIRECTED

This is the easiest of all decision-making processes in that someone directs you to make a specific decision. If it is your boss who is directing you regarding the decision, that's fine, because your boss may be informed and knowledgeable on software selection. On the other hand, if it is a third party, such as a salesperson, who is directing you toward the decision, you may not be making the best decision. Many people in the software selection process are swayed so extensively by salespeople that they are, in fact, directed by that salesperson into making a specific decision. Comments by the salesperson may be:

- If I were in your shoes I would buy this package.

- We have sold lots of them and the customers have been satisfied.

- It's the best piece of software on the market.

You can also be directed by friends or evaluations that you receive from other third parties. Many people use this method because they lack sufficient experience to use the judgment, and are unaware of other selection processes. If you are going to make a bad decision about selecting software, at least let it be your own bad decision.

METHOD 3 - QUALITATIVE

This method picks one or more attributes of software as the key selection element. It is selected software attributes that become the deciding factors. The qualitative method is a variation of the judgment method. The major difference is that in the qualitative method the characteristics that are evaluated through judgment are defined.

The more common qualitative characteristics included in software decision-making are:

- Vendor reputation
- Cost of software
- Promise of assistance
- Ease of acquisition

This can be a good decision-making process if sufficient software characteristics are defined, and the time and effort is taken to really evaluate and compare those qualities. When this method is used, the basis for the decision is known. The disadvantage is only when inadequate time is expended on defining, measuring, and comparing the qualities used in the decision-making process.

METHOD 4 - QUANTITATIVE

The quantitative method develops a score for each of the software packages being evaluated. This is the recommended method because it helps the inexperienced computer user make a decision free of the pressures and advice provided by third parties, particularly salespeople.

The quantitative evaluation decision-making process is used heavily throughout industry. Most employee pay grades in medium to large corporations are established through a quantitative scoring method. The skills required for that job are assigned a value, the value is accumulated and the total score translated into a pay grade. Major corporations use a scoring method for selecting sites for their factories or sales districts. Some corporations evaluate employee performance by assigning so many points for different areas of performance and then accumulating those points. The number of points received decide the amount of raise the employee will receive. Of course, schools and universities have been using the scoring system for centuries.

The scoring system suggested in this book is based upon the evaluation made in Step 4. During that step, you rated each of the criteria for each of the software candidates on how well that software package met the criteria. In the quantitative evaluation method we will accumulate those values to develop a score on which we will base our software solution decision.

> **SOFTWARE SELECTION SURVIVAL RULE #19**
> One of life's perplexing problems is living with
> a bad decision made for you by another person. Don't
> let that happen with the software selection decision.

DEVELOPING A SOFTWARE SELECTION SCORE

Developing the score is an easy exercise. The process begins when the software selection worksheet has been completed. The process will vary depending on whether only one software package is being evaluated or whether two or more are being compared.

Evaluating A Single Software Candidate

If only one software package has been located, the assessment process determines whether or not that software package is acceptable. If not, the last task in the evaluation process must determine the alternative to be used. The decision-making process involves the following tasks:

- o   Task 1 - Required requirements met - If the required requirements are not met by the software package being evaluated, it is unacceptable for selection, and you should proceed to Task 3 for determining an alternate solution.

- o   Task 2 - Assess evaluation - If all the needed requirements are met, the package is acceptable, and may or may not be selected. Reasons for nonselection may be that most of the high priority desired requirements are not present and without some or all of those the computer solution is not attractive at the price of the software. You may want to go through the scoring process described in the section dealing with evaluating more than one software package to determine whether the software falls above or below the average acceptability based on the prioritization of desired criteria.

If the software is acceptable, purchase it, and then read Chapter 9 on how to install and operate software. If the software does not appear to be worth the cost in resources to install and operate it, go to Task 3 and consider alternatives.

o Task 3 - Alternative solutions - If the software package is not acceptable, you have the following four alternative options to consider:

1) Look for other software packages - Review Step 2 of the selection process to help identify additional software candidates.

2) Process the work manually - Continue using existing manual processing methods, or develop manual processing methods to do the desired work.

3) Reevaluate criteria - Reconsider the importance of the criteria that the software package failed to

achieve. It may be that to gain the power of the computer, and to get the process automated, you can live without some of the desired features in anticipation of improved software becoming available within the foreseeable future.

4) Write your own software - Assumes you have adequate skills and sufficient time.

Evaluating Two or More Software Alternatives

When more than one software package is evaluated, a method is needed to select the best of the packages being evaluated. Developing a score is suggested. Figure 18 is a worksheet for this process. You use one column (i.e., numbered 1, 2, 3, and 4) for each software package being evaluated. The process is explained below:

- Task 1 - Needed requirements - If the needed requirements are not met, eliminate those software packages from the selection and scoring process.

- Task 2 - Total rating by assessment category - For each of the software packages being evaluated, accumulate the number of criteria rated in each of the four rating categories (i.e., fully satisfactory, satisfactory, less than satisfactory, and unsatisfactory) and put that number in Figure 18. For example, if three criteria were rated satisfactory, then for that software package a three would be put in the number (#) column for the satisfactory rating in Figure 18. This process continues until the total number of ratings in each assessment category for each software package is recorded on the software selection scoring worksheet (Figure 18).

o   Task 3 - Develop assessment score - Each of the four categories are then multiplied by a different value in order to give more weight to the fully satisfactory assessment than to the less than satisfactory assessment. The weights are as follows:

- Fully satisfactory = 3 points
- Satisfactory = 2 points
- Less than satisfactory = 1 point
- Unsatisfactory = 0 points

The score in each rating assessment category is developed by multiplying the number of times that category was picked in assessing the evaluation criteria for that software package. For example, if for software package 1 you had rated five criteria as fully satisfactory, then the fully satisfactory score for software package 1 would be fifteen. This score of fifteen is developed by multiplying the five fully satisfactory ratings times the value three points to develop a score of fifteen. This process continues for each of the categories and each of the software packages.

Figure 18/Software Selection Scoring Worksheet

RATING ASSESSMENT	SOFTWARE PACKAGE							
	1		2		3		4	
	#	SCORE	#	SCORE	#	SCORE	#	SCORE
Fully Satisfactory Multiply # by 3								
Satisfactory Multiply # by 2								
Less than Satisfactory Multiply # by 1								
Unsatisfactory Does not get any selection points								
TOTAL SCORE								

When all of the individual scores have been developed, they are then accumulated by software package. For example, for software package 1 the three scores developed for fully satisfactory, satisfactory, and less than satisfactory would be totaled and the total score put in the total score box at the bottom of the software package 1 score column.

o   Task 4 - Select a winner - The software package receiving the highest total score should be selected to solve your processing requirements. Note that if there is a tie, or two scores are very close, for example, within one to four points, you should consider using the following tiebreaking process in the order listed below:

- Tiebreaker #1 - Select the lowest cost software package.

- Tiebreaker #2 - Select the software package for which you think the vendor will provide the most service and assistance.

- Tiebreaker #3 - Select the software package for which the vendor has promised new versions and/or enhancements.

- Tiebreaker #4 - Flip a coin.

Buying the Software Package

The actual purchase of the software is normally an easy process. You may be asked for certain proprietary packages to sign a software agreement, but that is rare. Normally, you pay your money and take the software.

For your own protection, and to ensure minimal problems, be sure you know the answer to the following questions before you conclude the transaction:

1) Does the vendor guarantee that the software package will work as advertised, and if not, will it be replaced or repaired?

2) Can the software package be copied for backup purposes, and if not, does it have a self-destruct process embedded in the software?

3) If an improved version of the software package is released by the software vendor, can you acquire that package, and if so, at what price?

4) If you have trouble getting the package operational, who will help you make it work?

> **SOFTWARE SELECTION SURVIVAL RULE #20**
> Don't buy based on promises; buy based on facts. Promises have way of being forgotten or broken; facts have a longer life.

9
LEARNING AND INSTALLING SOFTWARE

I can't believe I bought a software package!

So now you own a software package. You have made the selection, you've got the software, and you've got whatever instructions or material the vendor provided you with. Now comes the agony and the ecstasy as you begin to use your software.

This chapter is designed to lead you through those first few exciting and sometimes frustrating hours as you put your software into use. Step-by-step work programs are included for both installing the software program on your computer system and for a shakedown exercise as you learn how to use the software effectively.

LOADING YOUR PROGRAM ONTO THE SYSTEM

When you first acquire a computer, it comes complete with an operating system and a library of programs. These may be programs included within the cost of the hardware, or they may be programs that you purchased in conjunction with the purchase of the computer hardware.

The method of initially starting your system, sometimes called an initial program load (IPL), boot, or some other term, is a process specified by the hardware manufacturer. Normally this process involves turning the power on, loading a diskette, and pushing one or two buttons on the terminal console. This will give you your initial screen which then leads you to the program or process that you want to perform.

If the program that you want to use is already in the program library, you only have to indicate which program you want. This is normally accomplished by indicating on a menu the program or process that you want. After you have selected a program, that program appears and you are ready to commence processing.

If your program is not on the computer, but is a new program, then the process is more complicated. Unless the program comes with the operating system, you will have to load the new program into your program library before you can begin to access and use the program. This process varies from computer to computer but basically involves the following tasks:

- o   Task 1 - Locate the operating system feature to load the new programs in the program library.

- o   Task 2 - Place the diskette with the new program on the second disk drive.

- o   Task 3 - Move the program from the second disk drive to the program library on the disk drive containing the operating system.

o   Task 4 - Call for the program through the operating system menu features and begin execution.

Two additional considerations need to be addressed during the program load process. These considerations are backup and security. Backup involves the storage of the program for use in the event the primary source of programs or data is lost. Security involves the protection of both the programs and the data from individuals who are not authorized to use those programs or data.

Security Considerations

The security of a minicomputer, its programs and data, is dependent upon the importance of the processing performed on that minicomputer. Obviously, the more important the information, the greater the need for security procedures. In a microcomputer environment security is physical security unless the microcomputer is connected via telephone lines to another computer. In that case, both physical and logical security are needed.

The programs and data in a microcomputer can be made physically secure by:

o   Keep the computer and all the records in a secure area of a building.

o   At the completion of processing, place all diskettes in a secure area, preferably locked.

o   Lock and protect operating instructions, printed reports, and carbon paper in accordance with the security requirements of the installation.

If the microcomputer is connected by telephone lines to other computers, the following security measures can be invoked:

o   Require identification of the user on the computer at the other end of the telephone line. If it is a dial-up network you can place the call. If the call is incoming and you are unsure of who is at the other end, disconnect and call back to the appropriate phone number.

o   Remove secure information from the disk drives when the system is in an on-line processing mode.

Backup Considerations

If you don't know now you will shortly that it is important to keep duplicate copies of all important data on electronic media. At a minimum, this should include:

o   Duplicate copies of the operating systems and all programs

o   Duplicate copies of files after an extended period of processing

It is also helpful to keep some backup data and programs in a location other than where the computer is stored. If that building should be destroyed by fire, flood, etc., the data and programs would still be available if they are stored in another physical location. A safe deposit box in a bank is a good safe storage location.

The Program Load Work Program (Checklist 3) can be used as a guide for loading your program into the computer.

SHAKE DOWN THE NEW PROGRAM

The shakedown period is an opportunity for you to become "friendly" with the software package. The equivalent with a new automobile is when you take it for a short drive to learn how the car handles, how the accelerator and brake feels, and to gain your confidence in driving a new car. Insurance company statistics show that a very high proportion of the automobile accidents occur in automobiles in which the driver has driven less than 100 miles. In other words, until the driver becomes confident in the use of the car they are much more susceptible to accidents. The same is true of computer software.

The tasks that an individual should perform in becoming friendly with computer software are:

    o   Task 1 - Read instructions

        The user of software should take sufficient time to gain an understanding of the software's capabilities and limitations.

CHECKLIST 3

PROGRAM LOAD WORK PROGRAM

#	ITEM	STEP PERFORMED		COMMENTS
		YES	NO	
1.	Turn computer on and initiate operating system.			
2.	If the program is on the operating system, locate program and commence processing. If not, complete items 3 through 8.			
3.	Place diskette with program on second disk drive.			
4.	Locate operating system feature to load program.			
5.	Initiate operating system process to load program from the second disk drive to the one on which the operating system is located.			
6.	Complete load steps as outlined in the operating system manual.			

CHECKLIST 3

(cont'd)

#	ITEM	STEP PERFORMED		COMMENTS
		YES	NO	
7.	Allocate disk space for use by the program if applicable.			
8.	Make a backup copy of the operating system diskette containing a new program. At a later time, verify that the copied diskette performs properly, and if so you can reuse the previous operating system backup diskette or move it to an off-site location.			

Note that this may have been done during the demonstration in which you were attempting to decide whether or not to acquire the software.

o   Task 2 - Review menus

A method you can use to become familiar with the capabilities of the software is to review the menus included in the software. The process begins by studying the capabilities contained in the first menu, from which you should select another menu, and so on until you have seen and analyzed all of the software menus.

o   Task 3 - Process a few typical transactions

Before you begin any live processing using the software, process a few test transactions. Make up a transaction and manually calculate the processed result. Then process that test transaction. Compare the result the computer produces versus the result you manually calculated. If there are differences, investigate the cause of the difference.

o   Task 4 - Create errors

It is important to understand what happens when you make a mistake in processing. Deliberately enter invalid data, attempt to delete data that should not be deleted, etc. Learn how the system reacts to these error conditions and what you must do to correct the condition.

o   Task 5 - Analyze report information

Through the processing of test transactions, create all of the major output reports. Make sure that you understand each field on the report, how it was calculated, and the relationship between the values in the reports.

o   Task 6 - Retrieve data

Store data in the computer files and retrieve that data. This will teach you the methods of inquiry, and through testing ensure that you know how to perform the retrieval task properly.

o   Task 7 - Cycle the system through two or more iterations

If a system produces payroll, then run payroll for two or more pay periods to ensure that the accumulation routines work properly.

o   Task 8 - Verify the functioning of controls

Identify the controls and perform sufficient processing to ensure the controls function properly.

Learning to Use the Software Work Program

The Learning to Use the Software Work Program (Checklist 4) provides a list of items that should be accomplished during the software shakedown. This list is an expansion of the above tasks, and is designed to be used to ensure that all the necessary steps are performed. At the end of the shakedown exercise, you should understand the functioning of the software, and feel confident in its use.

USE YOUR SOFTWARE

There are many reasons not to get a computer, not to acquire software, not to test it, and not to use it. However, it is the thing done that counts, not the plans and the thoughts of things to be.

The world is full of starters, but there are few finishers. Many people think that all man needs in initiative. But that is only one step. Action must be sustained to be effective. Many ideas are started, but few are finished.

Don't wait for the world to make better computers or build better software. There is no better software in the world at the current time than what exists. Acquire software, use it, and start enjoying the benefits of computer processing today.

CHECKLIST 4

LEARNING TO USE THE SOFTWARE WORK PROGRAM

#	ITEM	RESPONSE		COMMENTS
		YES	NO	
1.	Have you made a backup copy of the software application program?			
2.	Have you read and understood the instruction manual?			
3.	Have you displayed and become familiar with the software menus?			
4.	Have you created test transactions and manually determined the processing results for those transactions?			
5.	Have you entered data into the application system?			

CHECKLIST 4

(cont'd)

#	ITEM	RESPONSE YES	RESPONSE NO	COMMENTS
6.	Have you created errors in the data validation entry such as:			
	a) Values too large for the field			
	b) Improper codes			
	c) Used codes that don't exist in the computer			
	d) Used unreasonable values			
7.	Have you made a mistake in processing in order to understand the error correction process?			
8.	Have you tried the help routines?			
9.	Have you processed test transactions and verified the correctness of the results?			
10.	Do you understand all of the data in the output reports?			

CHECKLIST 4

(cont'd)

#	ITEM	RESPONSE YES	RESPONSE NO	COMMENTS
11.	Have you run the application through several sequences to ensure that the totaling routines function properly?			
12.	Have you attempted to retrieve data from the the transaction files?			
13.	Have you verified that the application controls function properly?			
14.	Have you allocated adequate space for both permanent data and transaction files?			
15.	Have you made provisions to back up the transaction data files?			
16.	If security procedures are needed, have you tested them, and are they adequate?			

SOFTWARE SELECTION SURVIVAL RULE #21
If you made a bad mistake in the software selection process eat your mistake and then acquire the proper package. Don't throw more time and money down the bad software rathole.

APPENDIX A
SOFTWARE VENDOR DIRECTORY

Advanced Operating Systems, 450 St. John Rd., Michigan City, IN 46360, (219) 879-4693

Altos Computer Systems, 2360 Bering Dr., San Jose, CA 95131, (408) 946-6700

American Business Systems, 459 Littleton Rd., Westford, MA 01886, (617) 692-2600

Apple Computer Co., 20525 Monani Ave., Cupertino, CA 95014, (408) 996-1010   Call

Applied Software Technology, 14125 Capri Dr., Los Gatos, CA 95030, (408) 370-2662

BPI Systems, Inc., 3423 Guadalupe, Austin, TX 78705, (512) 454-2801

Business Enhancement Compuservice, 1711 E. Valley Pkwy, Suite 109, Escondida, CA 92027, (714) 741-6335

Charles Mann & Assoc., 7594 San Remo Trail, Yucca Valley, CA 92284, (714) 365-9718

Cincom Systems, Inc., 2300 Montana Ave., Cincinnati, OH 45241, (513) 891-6647

CMS Software Systems, Inc., 2204 Camp David, Mesquite, TX 75149, (214) 285-3581

Compumax, P.O. Box 7239, Menlo Park, CA 94025, (415) 854-6700

Computer Products International, 3225 Danny Park, Computer Plaza Building, Metairie, LA 70002, (504) 455-5330

Computer Systems Design, P.O. Box 735, Yakima, WA 98902, (509) 453-2956

H. & E. Computronics, 50 N. Pascack Rd., Spring Valley, NY 10977, (914) 425-1535

Context, 23864 Hawthorne Blvd., Torrance, CA 90505, (213) 378-8277

Continental Software, 12101 Jefferson Blvd., Culver City, CA 90230, (213) 417-8031

Countryside Data Inc., 718 N. Skyline #201Q, Idaho Falls, ID 83402, (208) 529-8576

Cyma Corporation, 1550 E. University, Mesa, AZ 85203, (602) 835-8880

Dakin 5 Corp., P.O. Box 21187, Denver, CO 80221, (800) 525-0463

Data Train, Inc., 840 NW 6th St., Suite 3, Grant's Pass, OR 97526, (503) 476-1467

Denver Software Co., 36 Steele St., Suite 19, Denver, CO 80206, (303) 750-9980

Designer Software, 3400 Montrose Blvd. Suite 718, Houston, TX 77006, (713) 520-8221

Digital, 146 Main St., Maynard, MA 01574, 1-800-digital

Discount Software, 6520 Selma Ave., Suite 309, Los Angeles, CA 90028, (213) 837-5141

DYNACOMP, 1427 Monroe Ave., Rochester, NY 14618, (716) 425-2833

800-Software, Inc., 185 Berry St., Suite 6820, San Francisco, CA 94107, (800) 622-0678

GPS, 123 N. 15th, Fargo, ND 58102, (701) 293-8483

Graham-Dorian Software Systems, Inc., P.O. Box 16355, Fort Worth, TX 76133, (817) 294-5042

The Happy Computer, 460 N. Woodward Ave., Birmingham, MI 48011, (313) 644-8921

Howard Software Services, 8008 Girard Ave., Suite 310, LaJolla, CA 92037, (714) 454-0121

Innovative Business Software, 710 Williams Way, Richardson, TX 75080, (214) 699-9058

Inter-Care, 2044 Armacost Ave., Los Angeles, CA 90025, (213) 826-4500

International Micro Systems, 6445 Metcalf, Shawnee Mission, KS 66202, (913) 677-1137

Lear Data, 3273 Claremont Way, Suite 202, Napa, CA 94558, (707) 252-7139

Lifeboat Associates, 1651 Third Ave., New York, NY 10028, (212) 860-0300 call

Link Systems, 1640 19th St., Santa Monica, CA 90404, (213) 453-1851

Management Accountability Group, 493 E. Clayton St., Athens, GA 30603, (404) 353-8090

Micro-Architect, Inc., 96 Dothan St., Arlington, MA 02174, (617) 643-4713

Micro Business Software, Inc., Dover Rd., Willow Hill Bldg., Chichester, NH 03263, (603) 798-5700

Microcomputer Consultants, P.O. Box T, Davis, CA 95617,
(916) 756-8104

Micro-Ed, 3910 Bandini St., San Diego, CA 92103,
(714) 299-1125

Microhouse, 1444 Linden St., P.O. Box 498, Bethlehem, PA 18016,
(800) 523-9511

Micro Lab, 2310 Skokie Village Rd., Highland Park, IL, (312) 433-7550

Micromedia Marketing, Inc., 61 South Lake Ave., P.O. Box 4509,
Pasadena, CA 91106-0509, (213) 795-9646

Microsoft Corp., 10700 Northrup Way, Bellevue, WA 98004,
(800) 426-9400

Monroe Systems for Business, The American Road, Morris Plains, NJ
07950, (201) 540-7300

Mountain Computer, Inc., 300 El Pueblo Rd., Scotts Valley, CA 95006,
(408) 438-6650

Muse Software, 347 N. Charles St., Baltimore, MD 21201,
(301) 695-7212

National Software Systems, P.O. Box 510911, Salt Lake City, UT
84151, (208) 522-3592

NEC Home Electronics USA, 1401 Estes Ave., Elk Grove Village, IL 60007, (312) 228-5900

North Star Computers, 1440 4th St., Berkeley, CA 94710, (415) 357-8500

Panasonic Company, One Panasonic Way, Secaucus, NJ 07094, (201) 348-7000

Peachtree Software, 3 Corporate Sq., Atlanta, GA 30329, (404) 325-8533

Plus Computer Technology, Inc., 6900 North Austin Ave., Chicago, IL 60648, (800) 323-4240

Prodigy Systems, Inc., 497 Lincoln Highway, Iselin, NJ 08830, (415) 479-0600

QED Information Sciences, Inc., 170 Linden Street, Wellesley, MA 02181, (800) 343-4848

Quark Engineering, 1433 Williams, Suite 1102, Denver, CO 80218, (303) 399-1096

Quest, Inc., Suite B-30, Professional Center Pkwy, San Rafael, CA 94903, (415) 479-0600

Radio Shack, One Tandy Center, Forth Worth, TX 76102, (817) 390-3011

Sensible Software, 6619 Perham Dr., Dept. PC, West Bloomfield, MI 48033, (313) 399-8877

Sierra National Corp., 5037 Ruffner St., San Diego, CA 92111, (714) 277-4810

Small Business Computer Systems, 4140 Greenwood Ave., Lincoln, NE 68504, (402) 467-1878

Small Business Systems Group, 6 Carlisle Rd., Westford, MA 01886, (617) 692-3800

Softsel, 8295 S. La Cienega Blvd., Inglewood, CA 90301, (800) 421-5770

SoftwareBanc, One Faneuil Hall Marketplace, Boston, MA 02109, (617) 641-1241

Software Dimensions, Inc., 6371 Auburn Blvd., Citrus Heights, CA 95610, (916) 722-8000

Software Distribution Services, 1280 Main St., Buffalo, NY 14209, (800) 828-7250

Software Distributors, 9929 Jefferson Blvd., Culver City, CA 90230, (800) 421-0814

Software Hows, P.O. Box 36275, Los Angeles, CA 90036, (213) 829-6782

Software Publishing Corp., 1901 Landings Dr., Mountain View, CA 94043, (415) 962-8910

Software Technology for Computers, Inc., P.O. Box 428, Belmont, MA 02178, (617) 923-4334

Solid Software, Suite 501, 5500 Interstate North Parkway, Atlanta, GA 30328

Standard Software Corp. of America, 10 Mazzeo Drive, Randolph, MA 02368, (800) 343-0852

Star Computer Systems, 18051 Crenshaw Blvd., Torrance, CA 90504, (213) 538-2511

State of The Art, 3183-A Airway Ave., Costa Mesa, CA 92626, (714) 850-0111

Stoneware, Inc., 50 Belvedere St., San Rafael, CA 94901, (415) 454-6500

Structured Systems Group, 5204 Claremont, Oakland, CA 94618, (415) 547-1567

Systems Plus Inc., 1120 San Antonio Rd., Palo Atto, CA 94303, (415) 969-7047

Taranto & Assoc., P.O. Box 6073, San Rafael, CA 94903, (415) 472-2670

Taurus Software, 870 Market St., Suite 815, San Francisco, CA 94102, (415) 788-0888

TCS Software, Inc., 3209 Fondren Rd., Houston, TX 77063, (713) 977-7505

TeleVideo Systems, Inc., Dept. #623B, 1170 Morse Ave., Sunnyvale, CA 94086, (214) 258-6776

Texas Instruments, P.O. Box 225474, Dallas TX 75265, (214) 995-2011

Tiny Systems, Inc., 660 N. Glenville, Richardson, TX 75081, (214) 699-0261

Univar International, 10327 Lambert, International Airport, St. Louis, MO 63145, (314) 426-1099

User's Software, 7812 White Oak Ave., Northridge, CA 91325, (213) 708-8537

VANDATA, Suite 205, 17544 Midvale Ave. N., Seattle, WA 98133, (206) 542-7611

Videx, Inc., 897 N.W. Grant Ave., Corvallis, OR 97330, (503) 758-0521

Westico, 25 Van Zant St., Norwalk, CO 06855, (203) 853-6880

To Stuart
   Menu.

1. Company Information:
2. G/L Account Maintenance
3. Transaction Entry
4. Transaction Posting
5. Reports Menu
6. End of Period Procedures